Praise for *40 Days, 40 Ways to Pray*

"In a world filled with confusion and mixed messaging, I've had a front-row seat to Jonah Soucy's sharing the gospel through both his music and his ministry in a way that clearly resonates with adults and teens. Passionate about the Catholic Faith, he's a man of deep spirituality. In this book, he provides the reader with his lived experience on how to truly be in a relationship with our Lord and Savior. His writing is relatable, and his teachings are practical. A must-read for anyone looking to grow in Christ."

— ***Mark Joseph,*** Former Vice President for Evangelization and Renewal, Franciscan University of Steubenville

"Jesus departed from His disciples to be alone with His Father in prayer, and so, too, does every human being share this deepest of needs. This beautifully written book is full of wisdom and inspiration, and its author is an expert guide. Today, more than ever, we need ready access to our full inheritance of Catholic prayer. Jonah Soucy opens up these forms of Catholic prayer, allowing us an opportunity to try them out and find ways of prayer that fit our uniqueness as individual children of the Father. If you are a beginner, or if you're struggling with consistency in your prayer, I cannot recommend this book enough."

— ***Dr. James Pauley,*** Professor of Theology and Catechetics, Franciscan University of Steubenville; Author; Editor, *Catechetical Review*

"Jonah Soucy has authored a practical guide to deepening our relationship with the God who created us in love and redeemed us in Jesus Christ. This succinct yet substantive survey of thoughtful ways to pray and reflect on the mysteries of faith in the Catholic tradition are accessible to anyone seeking to journey with the heart of the Church during the holy season of Lent. *40 Days, 40 Ways to Pray* is a treasury of saintly wisdom and timeless devotion, with poignant reflections and spiritual questions to help make the Lenten journey intentional and fruitful. This Lent, as the Church directs the faithful to engage in the three-fold program of action — prayer, fasting, and almsgiving — let this book be your companion."

— ***Msgr. Anthony R. Frontiero, S.T.D.,*** Vicar General and Moderator of the Curia, Archdiocese for the Military Services, USA

"*40 Days, 40 Ways to Pray* is a transformative guide for anyone seeking to deepen their prayer life and grow closer to God. With its practical and approachable structure, this book invites readers into a forty-day journey of discovery, offering a basic theology of prayer while introducing a rich variety of methods drawn from the Church's spiritual heritage. Jonah Soucy masterfully combines timeless wisdom with actionable insights, making this an ideal resource for seasoned prayer warriors and those just beginning to explore the depths of prayer. By the end of the forty days, readers will have cultivated a more profound relationship with God and gained tools to sustain a vibrant, life-giving relationship with our Father."

— ***David Rinaldi,*** President, NET Ministries

40 Days, 40 Ways to Pray

Jonah Paul Soucy

40 Days, 40 Ways to Pray

SOPHIA INSTITUTE PRESS
Manchester, New Hampshire

Cover by Updatefordesign Studio
Cover image: Pastor hands in prayer position by deibyvargas (Freep!k 56084660)

Interior Images: Virgin of the Passion (Wikimedia Commons);
Scapular and Miraculous Medal by Deidre Folley

Sophia Institute Press
Box 5284, Manchester, NH 03108
1-800-888-9344
www.SophiaInstitute.com

Sophia Institute Press® is a registered trademark of Sophia Institute.

paperback ISBN 979-8-88911-254-9

ebook ISBN 979-8-88911-255-6

Library of Congress Control Number: 2024952380

Second printing

This book is dedicated to all of the young people whom I have ministered to, along with their families. May you always remember the love of God, and keep His heart close to your own.

CONTENTS

Acknowledgments

FIRST, I'D LIKE to thank both of my parents for raising me in the Catholic Faith, especially my mom who served as my first youth minister. Thanks for teaching me how to pray, Mom. I'd also like to thank my wife, Shannon, for allowing me to spend so many late nights working on this book. You are forever the greatest gift God has ever blessed me with. Thanks for being my best friend.

From a formative perspective, there are so many individuals who played a role in my spiritual growth that it would be impossible to name them all. Parents of friends, youth ministers, and Core Team members who invested their life and their time in me: please know that I am so grateful for you. In the same vein, I'd like to thank the people at Lifeteen, NET Ministries, Preambula Group, my professors at Franciscan University, and the past and present staff at the Steubenville Conference Office (especially Mark Joseph) for the formative experiences that you have all provided for me at various points of my life. You all do wonderful work building up the kingdom of God. I'd also like to thank my college household and brotherhood, the Knights of the Holy Queen, the greatest group of men I could ever ask to spend my college years with. I must especially thank Diego Araujo, my fellow knight, roommate, and best man. Diego was the first to plant the seed in my mind that everyone's relationship with God is unique and unrepeatable, and therefore everyone's way of speaking and listening to God was unique. I'd also like to thank the parishioners and staff at St. Matthew and Triumph of the Holy Cross Parishes, especially those whom I've had the honor of serving alongside in ministry. It is a joy serving you all.

I am also immensely indebted to everyone over at Sophia Press. Thank you for believing in this book enough to bring it to life! I'd especially like to thank my editor, Laura Bement, whose contributions greatly improved the quality of this work, as well as Anna Maria Dube, Charlie McKinney, Bob Land, Sarah Lemieux, Jennah Costa, and everyone else who helped bring this book to fruition and share it with the world.

Finally, and most importantly, I'd like to thank and praise God from whom every blessing flows. In Him we live and move and have our being. How blessed we are, to be called children of God.

Welcome!

HELLO, AND THANKS so much for picking up this book! I'm so glad that you are here, and I hope that in the coming days you are able to draw closer to God and experience Him and His love for you in a more powerful way.

The goal of this book is to help you discover methods and forms of prayer that allow you to connect more deeply to God. As you make your way through the forty different ways to pray, you will find that some of these engage your heart and mind more than others. That is a *good thing* and speaks to your particular and individual identity as a son or daughter of God. Since each of us is unique and unrepeatable, each of our relationships to God is unique and unrepeatable. The way that I pray is going to be different from the way that you pray. If something doesn't quite speak to you or help you reach a place of interior contemplation (peaceful resting in God's presence), it doesn't mean you are praying wrong; it could just be that this particular way of praying is not the one that helps you enter into prayer in this time of your life. With that being said, I always recommend coming back to different forms of prayer in different seasons of life. There are countless examples of ways to pray in this book that didn't really help me enter into prayer when I was younger but have really brought me a lot of spiritual fruit in recent years.

This book is written primarily as a forty-day prayer challenge. The idea is that you commit yourself to doing one of the forty chapters each day. Each chapter consists of a brief reflection on a method of prayer followed by an Action Step to accomplish before you start the next chapter and ideas for Going Deeper if you'd like to learn more about a particular method. This forty-day structure makes it perfect for the Lenten season, but this book really can be read at any time of the year by anyone looking to deepen their relationship with God.

You can read this book and undertake this prayer challenge on your own, but I highly recommend reading it with a partner or small group to help with accountability and processing the material. A quick daily check-in and sharing some thoughts can go a long way toward helping you engage with the material on a deeper level and experience God in communion with others.

It should be stated that even though this book was designed with this forty-day model in mind, you are free to use it however you would like! You can read multiple sections in a day, or if you find one particular method to be particularly fruitful, you can sit with it for weeks before moving on to the next one. You can also skip entire sections if you see something in the Table of Contents that captures your eye. As the reader, you have complete freedom to use this book in whatever way helps you grow closer to God. After all — that is the ultimate end to which this book is devoted! There really isn't a wrong way to use this book, as long as it is bearing fruit in your life and helping you deepen your relationship with the Lord. Anything that takes you away from that goal can be set aside.

As I mentioned above, each chapter of *40 Days, 40 Ways to Pray* comes with an Action Step to complete. Most of the time, this step asks you to attempt the actual method of prayer that is being discussed and to write briefly about your experience. Other times (especially in the Christian Essentials part of the book), it involves scheduling time in the future for prayer. Sometimes this action step has you respond to a writing prompt of some sort or encourage you to step outside your comfort zone. The full-freedom rule applies here as well, but I do encourage you to stretch yourself during these forty days!

Finally, as you make your way through the book, be sure to write down anything that stands out to you or anything you feel God may be trying to tell you through your prayer time, and whether you were able to engage your heart and enter a place of contemplation. That "invitation" to contemplation and that feeling of God's presence are often signs that God is inviting you to this particular prayer form in this season of your life. I also highly encourage you to write down which prayer methods you liked best so that you can come back and do a deeper dive into them after you finish the book.

General Tips for Prayer Time

When taking time for prayer, keep a few things in mind. Most importantly, I want to share the importance of actually taking scheduled prayer time — of *actually setting time aside* to communicate with and listen to God. Taking time in prayer will unlock depths of peace and grace that will amaze you to no end. I often hear people say, "I pray at scattered moments throughout the day. I don't really have a set time where I talk to God." Try applying this logic to any other intimate human relationship. For example, what would happen to your friendships if you never took time to respond when friends reach out to you or to spend any time with them? How would it strengthen your marriage if you scheduled more date nights? What you hopefully recognize is that *all relationships require invested quality time if they are to grow.* Our relationship with God is no different in that regard.

Another important point is that our posture matters! The reason for this is simple and rooted in the fact that our *bodies* matter. As human beings we are both body and soul. Praying as we are falling asleep in bed or slouched over can hinder us from fully entering into prayer. We should pray in a posture that communicates attentiveness with our whole bodies. Some of us may like to kneel; others may enjoy simply sitting in a comfortable manner on a couch or even sitting with your legs crossed on the floor. But generally, when going into an intentionally scheduled time of prayer, we want to avoid postures that put us in danger of falling asleep as well as any that make us feel too uncomfortable, maybe causing us to end our prayer time prematurely.

Because we are both body and spirit we also want to try and engage all of our bodily senses in our prayer time (or at least as many of them as we can). Sacred art or icons of Jesus, Mary, and the saints; blessed incense; holy water; sacred music — all of these can help contribute to an environment more conducive to prayerfully encountering God, not because they make Him any more present than He already is, but rather because they help to draw our attention and our hearts deeper into His presence.

Finally, it should be said that if you fall off the wagon and stop praying for a time, you can always try again. Shake off the dust and pick back up where you left off. God has a plan for your life, and that plan reveals itself most clearly when we take time with Him in prayer! But as Christians, we also have to be aware of the reality that there is an evil one who wants nothing more than to stop us from developing a deeper relationship with God. Step one of his plan is universal in its scope: keep us from praying, or if we are praying already, stop us from praying.

Distractions and temptations *will* begin to crop up when you begin to take prayer more seriously. But keep going! Even if you fall into serious sin or begin to slide into complacency, don't wait until you get to Confession to begin praying again. Sin wounds our hearts and our relationships with God, others, and ourselves. But the good news is this: nothing you've done can make God stop loving you, and our Father in heaven does not love us any less when we fall short. Moreover, when we turn back to God, He runs to us like the Father in the parable of the prodigal son, to embrace us and bring us back to spiritual life with Him (see Luke 15:11–32). As Jesus told St. Faustina, "The greater the sinner, the greater the right he has to my mercy."[1] Accept His love and His mercy. Allow Him to pick you up, and keep following Him; keep striving to encounter Him in prayer.

Please be assured of my prayers for you as you begin this journey. I hope that this book leads you closer to the heart of God the Father, and deeper into the life of the Holy Trinity. I also hope these forty days can be a sort of "retreat" for you, an experience of God's peace that draws you out of the mundane and into a deeper awareness of His presence.

Mother Mary, please wrap all of us in your mantle. Protect us from all attacks, temptations, and lies of the evil one, and through the power of your Immaculate Heart lead us closer to your Son, Jesus.

St. Joseph, pray for us.

All you holy angels and saints, pray for us. Amen.

1 *The Diary of Saint Maria Faustina Kowalska,* 3rd ed. (Stockbridge, MA: Marian Press, 2008), p. 292, entry 723.

40 Days, 40 Ways to Pray

PART 1

Introduction

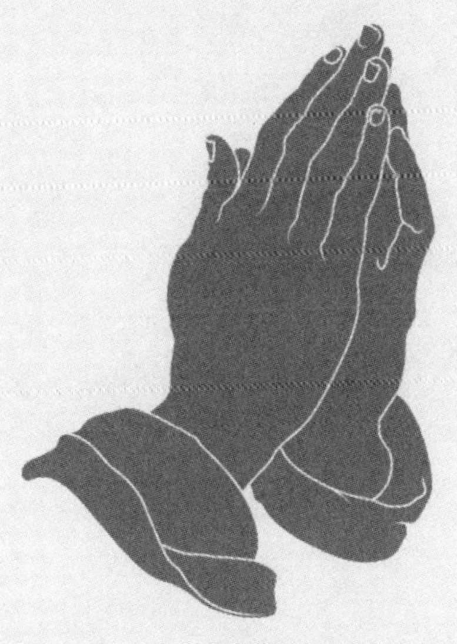

On these first two days, you will be learning the basics of Christian prayer. On the first day you'll learn a simple definition of prayer and what prayer consists of. On Day 2, we'll look at the three main expressions, or what I like to call "movements," of prayer. The purpose of this is to create a foundation that we can build upon throughout the rest of these forty days. Not only will you learn what Christian prayer is, but you will hopefully see why it is so important to experience life in the fullest sense.

Day 1

What Is Christian Prayer?

CHRISTIAN PRAYER, UNDERSTOOD in its most simple expression, is our personal relationship with God. God *desires* this personal relationship with you. When the Word became flesh and dwelt among us, He calls us friends (see John 15:15) and offers us life to the full (see John 10:10). The radical truth of Christianity is that the Father gave His own Son so that we can have eternal life, Jesus gave His own life on the Cross to reveal to us the depths of His love, and these depths of love are poured out in the Person of the Holy Spirit, who comes and dwells within us. Christian prayer, therefore, is "Trinitarian." It leads us deeper into the life of the Holy Trinity and helps us grow in relationship with God the Father, God the Son, and God the Holy Spirit.

In prayer, we penetrate the mystery of the Holy Trinity and enter into the inner relationship that exists between the Father, Son, and Holy Spirit. We drink of the water that quenches every thirst, and our own hearts become springs of living water. Prayer is not simply a time of quieting our thoughts or emptying our minds — it is an opportunity to become filled by divine life. This reality is made possible by the joint mission of the Son and the Spirit. Through the Incarnation, God took on human flesh, and as a result, human flesh receives a new capacity for God. As St. Athanasius famously put it, "God became man so that man might become like God."[2] Prayer also allows the fruits of the Spirit to grow deep roots in us, and we begin to experience these fruits in a real way: a deeper outpouring of love, joy, peace, patience, kindness, goodness, faithfulness, gentleness, and self-control in our minds, our hearts, and our relationships with others. Through the gift of the Spirit poured upon us, we become children of God, and our bodies become temples of the Holy Spirit. Prayer therefore changes us for the better and helps us live a life truly rooted in Christ.

All of this serves a singular purpose: that we can come to know and love God. This love enables us to serve His kingdom by spreading His love to others. As Scripture teaches us,

> For God is love. In this the love of God was made manifest among us, that God sent his only Son into the world, so that we might live through him. In this is love, not that we loved God but that he loved us and sent his Son to be the expiation for our sins. . . . By this we know that we abide in him and he in us, because he has given us of his own Spirit. And we have seen and testify that the Father has sent his Son as the Savior of the world. Whoever confesses that Jesus is the Son of God, God abides in him, and he in God. So we know and believe the love God has for us. God is love, and he who abides in love abides in God, and God abides in him. (1 John 4:8–10, 13–16, RSVCE)

When one takes time in prayer daily, these mysteries become revealed and one's heart and mind are transformed to be more like God, who is love. In prayer, we abide in Him and He abides in us.

[2] St. Athanasius, *On the Incarnation*, trans. John Behr, Popular Patristics (Yonkers, NY: St. Vladimir's Seminary Press, 2011), p. 107, entry 52 (paraphrase). It reads, "For he was incarnate that we might be made god."

Put in this light, we come to the realization that *a life without prayer is a life without this personal relationship*. A Christian who professes to believe in God but doesn't pray is like the older brother in the parable of the prodigal son. We remain in the house of the Father but we don't have His life flowing through us. The younger brother takes his inheritance and squanders it, but we settle for complacency and don't recognize the fullness of life that God wants to give us through a prayer relationship. Yet the Father reminds us, "You are always with me, and all that is mine is yours" (Luke 15:31–32, RSVCE). We receive our inheritance — the fullness of divine life — through prayer.

To put it another way: just as food, water, and rest are all nourishment to our bodies, prayer is nourishment for our souls. There is a longing inside each of us for the eternal and the divine. Unfortunately, instead of finding our fulfillment in God, we distract ourselves from our spiritual thirst and from the deepest longings of our hearts. We waste our leisure time with things like scrolling through social media, hobbies, and chasing power, riches, and pleasure. Instead of finding a peaceful solitude when we are alone, we experience isolation and uneasiness. When we do this, we have no clue how much we are missing out on. In the modern world, it has become all too easy to distract ourselves from the deepest longings of our hearts. We medicate and anesthetize our restlessness to avoid the unhappiness in the deepest places of our souls. Instead of being able to enjoy silence and stillness as a place of deep encounter and contemplation in the presence of God, we do everything we can to avoid it. But the age-old truth remains, "Our hearts find no peace until they rest (in Him)."[3] We find ourselves in an age where what we may call "restless

3 Augustine, *Confessions*, trans. and intro. R. S. Pine-Coffin (London: Penguin Books, 1961), p. 21, I.1.

heart syndrome" reigns supreme. Modern man has moved further and further away from God, and we have paid for it dearly. The reality is that we were made *by* God and *for* God. Nothing will satisfy the deepest longings of our hearts except for Him.

So how exactly do we begin to experience Him? How do we pray? The very first step of Christian prayer is simply speaking to God with your interior voice. St. Thérèse of Lisieux wrote of prayer, "Prayer, for me, is simply a raising of the heart, a simple glance toward Heaven, an expression of love and gratitude in the midst of trial, as well as in times of joy."[4] First, we quiet our minds and push aside distractions. We then acknowledge and become aware that God is present and listening. We bring whatever is on our hearts before God: trials and tribulations, joys and consolations, questions and concerns. All of it matters to Him. We then quiet ourselves to interiorly "listen" and next take time to rest. This form of freely speaking to God is often called "mental prayer," speaking and listening to God in our mind.

4 Thérèse of Lisieux, *Story of a Soul*, trans. Michael Day (Charlotte, NC: TAN Books, 2010), 141.

✎ Action Step ✎

TODAY, YOUR ACTION step is to take a few moments to attempt mental prayer. For many of you, this is going to feel totally foreign, but I encourage you to give it a shot. I also want to strongly encourage you to write a little bit about what you experience during this time. This practice of writing your reflections from your prayer time is called "prayer journaling," and it is a wonderful way to track your prayer journey. There will be times in your life when you come to prayer needing encouragement and you have a profound experience, and when you record these experiences, you will be able to see God at work over the course of your life. Your faith can then be strengthened when you read about and remember what God has done in your life.

The other reason to record your prayer time with God is that it helps you to take what is going on internally and externalize it through writing. This process actually helps what we experience stick in our mind more. Tomorrow we'll look at one possible way of structuring these thoughts a bit, but for today I simply invite you to reflect on the questions and areas of your life that you want to bring before the Lord. Sit in quiet and write down what you believe He is speaking to you. Use a notebook, prayer journal, or the space below to write about the experience.

____

____

____

____

____

Going Deeper

MANY WONDERFUL BOOKS out there serve as excellent introductions to prayer. Here are a few that have been really influential in my own life or in the lives of close friends of mine:

- *Prayer for Beginners* by Peter Kreeft
- *Time for God* by Fr. Jacques Philippe
- *Appointment with God* by Fr. Michael Scanlon
- *The Rhythm of Life* by Matthew Kelly
- *Personal Prayer: A Guide for Receiving the Father's Love* by Fr. Thomas Acklin and Fr. Boniface Hicks

Day 2

Three Expressions of Christian Prayer

In the Christian Tradition, prayer is broken up into three main movements or expressions of prayer: vocal prayer, meditative prayer, and contemplative prayer (CCC 2700–2719).

Vocal prayer is simply talking to God, either out loud or in our hearts and minds like we tried yesterday. Rote prayers that we have memorized, such as the Our Father or Hail Mary, are a popular way to pray vocally. Vocal prayer also includes singing or praying with a group in a prayer group setting or liturgical context. Praying out loud, especially with others, can help promote a sense of unity and connection. Vocal prayer can also help our hearts and our minds begin to quiet down and enter more deeply into prayer.

Meditative prayer (also called "meditation"), in a Christian context, refers to *thinking* about the things of God. The Catechism calls meditation a "quest," as our mind "seeks to understand the why and how of the Christian life" (CCC 2705). Meditation includes reading and studying Scripture or other spiritual books, praying with sacred art and icons, reflecting on the beauty of nature and creation, and studying God's actions and revelation in human history. This idea of meditation is very different from definitions of meditation that exist in other religions and even in a more secular sense nowadays. From these non-Christian perspectives, meditation means something like "clearing one's mind" using a combination of physical or mental techniques. But Christian meditation is a more active engagement of the mind as we strive to know and love God better.

If meditation is a quest toward God, contemplative prayer is what occurs when our hearts find what our minds were searching for. It is a prayer in which our heart rests in God's heart. It is spending time with God in the quiet, taking time to listen to Him. In the stillness, we allow God to work on our hearts. Contemplative prayer is what vocal prayer and meditation ultimately lead us to. It is looking at God and allowing Him to look into the recesses of our heart. It is training ourselves to listen to God and be at perfect peace and harmony with Him. It is silent adoration of our Lord, who has become fully present to us.

One can see that the more secular and modern notion of meditation is more akin to what Christians call "contemplation," but even here there is a key difference — at the center of contemplative prayer there is a Person, Jesus of Nazareth. There is certainly a psychological and emotional benefit to be had from many meditative practices, but the ultimate goal of contemplative prayer — and one that makes it so different from any other religious or secular meditative practice — is to become more deeply aware of a greater Presence who surrounds us and dwells within our hearts. We read in Scripture that the Word of God "emptied himself, taking the form of a slave." Theologians refer to this movement as the *kenosis,* the self-emptying of God. And so, in a sense, we imitate God when we empty ourselves as we pour out our hearts and minds in prayer. However, true Christian meditation is *not a movement away* from the self; it is primarily a movement of the mind and heart *toward* God.

When I give public talks about prayer, I often say that prayer consists of three major movements: *talking* to God (vocal prayer), *listening* to God (meditation), and *being* with God (contemplation).

A healthy prayer life consists of all three of these movements; each of the three expressions of prayer is vital for a healthy relationship with God. This makes perfect sense, as each of these is crucial for any other relationship in our life. The quality and depth of our relationships are based on how well we talk with, listen to, and spend time around each other.

Each expression of prayer is similar in that it must be led by the heart. But what, exactly, does this mean? Catholic philosopher Dietrich von Hildebrand defines the heart as one of the three "spiritual centers" in man, alongside the intellect and the will.[5] Our intellect is the center of our spiritual capacity to think and rationalize. Our will is the spiritual center of desire and the ability to give our assent to something. The heart is the affective center of man, the home for our spiritual capacity for emotions such as joy and love — the source of our ability to experience "being moved" when we encounter something profoundly beautiful or inspiring. In order to experience God to the fullest, we have to engage each of these three spiritual centers. We must know Him, desire Him, and love Him.

Therefore, engaging the heart means intentionally striving to fan into flames a deeper love and appreciation of God. I am not saying that we need to build our prayer relationship on our emotions, which can be fickle and change from moment to moment. We need to *allow ourselves* to be moved by our encounter with God just like we would allow ourselves to be moved by anything else of great beauty, of which God is the source.

When we pray with our voices, we shouldn't simply be rattling off rote prayers that we have memorized. The Our Father and the Hail Mary are beautiful prayers, but we need to engage our hearts as

[5] Dietrich von Hildebrand, *The Heart: An Analysis of Human and Divine Affectivity* ([1965] South Bend, IN: St. Augustine's Press, 2007).

well as our voices when we pray them. We need to foster an attentive interior disposition that says, *Lord, I am here and I want to experience your peace and love more in my life. I want to love you more.* Meditation is not simply mental exercise or stimulation; it is the heart seeking deeper understanding about the things of God in order that we can know Him and love Him better. Contemplation is not simply quiet time but time spent with our loving Father and with Jesus in the power of the Holy Spirit where our mind is able to rest, but our heart soars to new heights.

As you make your way through this book, you will learn many different forms of prayers that come from the Church's two thousand years of history. All of these traditions have two things in common: they can each be tied to all three of these expressions of prayer, and in each of them you should make the effort to engage the heart as much as possible. Allow yourself to be moved by the power and beauty of God. Ask Him for the grace to help you love Him and others more deeply. You should also pay attention as you pray to any moments in which you feel an invitation to rest your mind and enter into the deeper prayer of the heart. The temptation here is to keep chugging along with the vocal prayer that you are doing at the moment, but in reality this is an invitation to contemplation, which is the goal of all prayer! When this happens, I encourage you to put aside whatever vocal or meditative prayer you are doing and simply rest in Him for as long as you can before distractions arise. Then continue along in your vocal prayer or meditation until the invitation to contemplation returns.

✎ Action Step ✎

YOUR ACTION STEP today is to take a few minutes to talk to God in your mind again, but this time we'll be adding a little more structure to it. We'll be going through the three major movements that we spoke of in today's chapter, and we will also look at several types of prayer. To help navigate this process, we'll use an acronym: PRAY. Simple enough!

You can spend as little as thirty seconds on each of these steps, or you can dive in and really devote good chunks of quality time with each movement. What you pour in is often what you get out! But also remember that God speaks to us all differently. Some parts come more naturally to you than others. Use your journal or the space below each prompt to write down some things that come to mind in each of the steps.

> **Praise** — Take a few moments to praise God and thank Him for all of the incredible blessings in your life. Praise opens our hearts up to God and trains us to be grateful for all of life's little blessings. After you run out of things that you can think of, pause for a little while then try to think of five more! A grateful heart is a happy heart. During this time, we want to stir up in our hearts a sense of gratefulness and wonder at all that God has given us. (Vocal prayer)

____

____

____

____

Repent — Take some time to reflect back on the day, week, or however long it's been since you had some quality prayer time. Recognize that God has been with you in all of the moments of your life, and that there have been moments in which you have stepped away from Him or even rebelled against Him in sin. How do you need to get right with God? What do you have to repent for? Remember that repentance is a twofold movement; we move *away* from sin and *toward* God. In your own words or using an "Act of Contrition" (an example can be found in Appendix A), apologize for the areas in which you fell short, and ask God to help you not fall short in the same way again. Remember that there is nothing you have done that would make God stop loving you, and there is nothing that you can do to try and "earn" more of God's love. (Vocal and meditative prayer)

____

____

____

____

Ask — Now take some time to think of the areas of your life and the lives of those around you where divine assistance is needed. In your own words, ask God for help in those areas (vocal prayer). Also, spend time reflecting on what you think God would want you to pray for in your life, the lives of others around you, and on the world stage. Pray for these things as well. (Meditative prayer)

____

____

____

Yield — In this final step, simply give permission for God to work in your heart and your mind in whatever way He deems fit. Try to push aside distractions and other thoughts. Feel free to use a repetitive phrase such as "Come Holy Spirit," "Come Lord Jesus," "Speak, Father," or something akin to that to help quiet your mind. Make sure your body posture is one that will help you pray without growing too sleepy or too uncomfortable! Try and rest in this place of peace for a couple of minutes. Write a little bit about your experience below. (Contemplative prayer)

____

____

____

____

Going Deeper

TO LEARN MORE about Christian prayer, review the fourth section of the *Catechism of the Catholic Church,* which takes an in-depth look at the Christian prayer tradition. In doing so, you will learn more about what prayer truly consists of. You'll also learn more about the three expressions of Christian prayer as well as the main movements of mental prayer.

PART 2

Christian Essentials

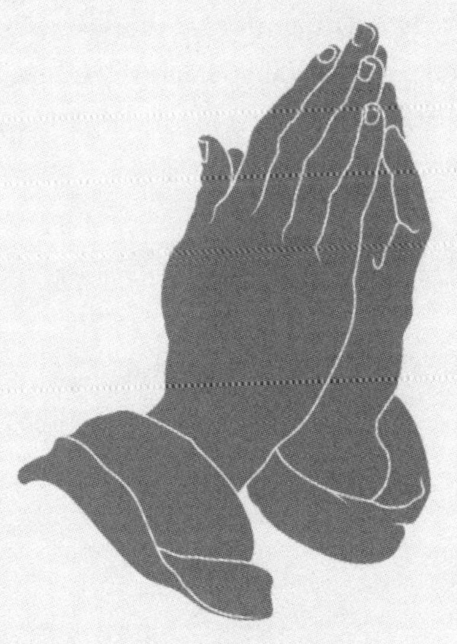

In this section, we're going to be talking about the *essential* forms of Christian prayer. The vast majority of the prayer expressions and spiritual practices found in this book really aren't obligatory. This section, however, deals with the things that should be incorporated into the life of every person who calls him- or herself a disciple of Jesus and wants to follow Him more closely. In other words, we are putting first things first. In addition to explaining what each of these essentials is, we also take a deeper look at *why* it is considered essential in the Christian life.

For many of the chapters in this section, it might not be practical to actually *do* the prayer on the day that you are reading about it. For example, if reading the chapter "Day 5" in the evening, there's a good chance that all of the options for Mass have passed for the day. That is quite alright! The Action Step for the day was written with this in mind. Some days, you will simply set time aside in the future to complete a prayer, but ensure that you actually follow through with each action step so that you can better learn about these beautiful forms of prayer and draw closer to God.

Day 3

The Sign of the Cross

HAVE YOU EVER wondered why many Christians make the sign of the Cross before and after they pray? From an outside perspective, it may seem strange. In many cases, especially in the modern world, it can even be reduced to a superstition — something used as a sort of good-luck charm, a rabbit's foot with a Christian twist.

The reality is that marking ourselves with the sign of the Cross traces its roots back into the days of the early Church, even as far back as the time of the apostles. St. Basil wrote that it came directly from the apostles' unwritten teaching.[6] This makes sense, considering that when Jesus commissioned the apostles in Matthew 28, He taught them to make disciples, "baptizing them *in the name of the Father and of the Son and of the Holy Spirit*" (Matt. 28:19, RSVCE, emphasis added). Moreover, in the original Greek, the preposition commonly translated as "in" is better translated as "into,"[7] which means that Baptism transfers us into the heart of communion between the Father, Son, and Holy Spirit. So when we make the sign of the Cross,

[6] St. Basil the Great, *On the Holy Spirit,* cited in Scott Hahn and Mike Aquilina, *Living the Mysteries: A Guide for Unfinished Christians* (Huntington, IN: Our Sunday Visitor Publishing Division, 2003), 38.

[7] Matthew 28:19b: εἰς τὸ ὄνομα τοῦ πατρὸς καὶ τοῦ υἱοῦ καὶ τοῦ ἁγίου πνεύματος.

we signify that we are entering into this communion and acknowledge our intention to draw deeper into the heart of God.

It may surprise you to learn that, throughout the Church's history, the sign of the Cross has had several variations. In the early Church, making the sign of the Cross consisted mostly in tracing the shape of the letter *T* on the forehead, lips, or breast — just like we do at Mass right before the reading of the Gospel when we ask that the Lord draw our minds, lips, and hearts closer to Him. Even today, there are differences in how people from different geographic areas use the sign of the Cross. For example, in some places the thumb, index finger, and middle finger of the hand are pinched together; in other places the palm is open. In some places, people cross themselves from left to right; in other places they go right to left. There is much diversity in practice, but the root remains the same. We make the sign of the Cross over ourselves as a way to draw ourselves deeper into the mystery of God.[8]

It's worth noting here that making the sign of the Cross also reveals something about our nature as human beings, namely the fact that we are both *body* and *soul*. We pray not only with our mind and spirit but with our bodies as well. Making the sign of the Cross acts as a psychological and physical reminder to center our attention more deeply into prayer, so when we make the sign of the Cross, we should do so prayerfully, full of intentionality.

We can use the sign of the Cross as we enter into or conclude formal prayer time. We can also use it spontaneously when we feel the need to remind ourselves of God's presence. Doing it with holy water, a sacramental that reminds us of our Baptism, can also be beneficial. We can trace the sign of the Cross over things as a sign of

[8] Bert Ghezzi, *Sign of the Cross: Recovering the Power of the Ancient Prayer* (Chicago: Loyola Press, 2004), 17–26.

blessing or simply inviting God in. We can trace it over the foreheads of our children and spouses, or even over our coffee mug, textbooks, or cell phone to remind us that all things should be used to glorify God. We can also make the sign of the Cross before a sporting event or big endeavor as a sensory reminder that God is always with us despite whatever outcome transpires. There really are countless ways that we can utilize this little prayer throughout the day to draw our attention back to God and remind us that every good thing we have comes from Him, and ultimately everything must return to Him.

Action Step

SLOWLY AND PRAYERFULLY make the sign of the Cross. Take some time today to brainstorm some ways you can incorporate the sign of the Cross more into your daily life. Several ideas were listed above, and I encourage you to think of some of your own. Write down some ideas in the space below and put them into practice in the coming days and weeks.

____

____

____

____

Going Deeper

IF YOU'D LIKE to learn more about the sign of the Cross and find more ways to incorporate it into your daily life, I recommend the book *Sign of the Cross: Recovering the Power of the Ancient Prayer* by Bert Ghezzi. You can find an excerpt from the book on the Word on Fire Blog.[9]

9 Bert Ghezzi, "A Short History of the Sign of the Cross," Word on Fire, January 13, 2023, https://www.wordonfire.org/articles/contributors/a-short-history-of-the-sign-of-the-cross/.

Day 4

Confessing Sin

IN THE BEGINNING of this book, I mentioned that prayer is our relationship with God. In any relationship, there are times when we are really thriving and doing a wonderful job loving the other person in the way they deserve. But the reality is that sometimes we mess up, miss the mark, or even cause harm to those we care about. God is the perfect lover and perfect friend who never abandons us. In fact, when we stray from Him and even when we cause Him and His children harm, He gives us a way back to Him through the process of confessing our sins in the Sacrament of Reconciliation.

In order to understand why this sacrament is so important, we first need to understand the reason it exists. In other words, we need to understand *sin.*

What Is Sin?

Over the centuries, the Church's theological understanding and conception of sin have deepened.[10] The early Church primarily understood sin as a debt toward God, and in the Middle Ages, the Church heavily emphasized the stain, burden, or weight of sin. In recent times, there has been an emphasis on sin as a wound. For example, Pope Francis recently commented, "Sin is more than a stain. Sin is a wound; it needs

[10] Gary Anderson, *Sin: A History* (New Haven, CT: Yale University Press, 2009), 3–39.

to be treated, healed."[11] And there is no better person to help us in our struggle against sin than Jesus, the Divine Physician: He doesn't just want to erase sin, He wants to *heal us* from it.

We are made in the image and likeness of God, and we were made for communion with Him and with one another. Sin is anything that spiritually wounds us or these relationships with God and others. It darkens our intellect, leads to disorder in our will, and desensitizes our hearts to the movements of God. This is the burden and stain that sin places on us. Moreover, because God is the source of goodness, whenever we commit a moral evil or fail to do a moral good when it is within our power to do so, we damage our relationship with God and our capacity for moral goodness. So when we choose sin, our relationship with God, others, or even ourselves is wounded, whether we recognize and acknowledge it.

Repeated sin also has the effect of numbing our conscience. The first time a particular sin is committed we may feel in our soul a sense of wrongness. We know in our heart of hearts that something is wrong, that something foreign to our soul has taken root. But if we do not bring this wrong into the light, the wound gets to work — numbing the voice of conscience within us like a sort of spiritual Novocain in our conscience. We start to feel numb to the wrongness of sin, and our consciences are weakened.

Finally, sin enslaves us. In the Gospel of John, Jesus tells us, "Truly, truly, I say to you, every one who commits sin is a slave to sin" (John 8:34, RSVCE). In other words, sin is addictive and leads to greater sin if we do not repent of it. When we freely consent to sin, we actually begin to *desire* sin more — even when it robs us of our peace and fails to bring about lasting happiness.

[11] Pope Francis, *The Name of God Is Mercy: A Conversation with Andrea Tornielli*, trans. Oonagh Stransky (New York: Random House, 2016), 26.

Our culture misunderstands freedom to mean choosing to do whatever we want, whenever we want, with whomever we want, and so many people believe that when they choose something contrary to the moral law, they are exercising their greatest right to freedom. However, this view of freedom is incredibly limiting, and it is contrary to the true spiritual freedom that God wants for us. True freedom consists in being able to do what is good, even when it is difficult. We merit this ability to choose the good by *cooperating* with God's grace to live a more perfect life. We put time and energy into prayer and our faith so that God may transform us and perfect us in His love. Jesus desires true spiritual freedom for us because He desires for us to be happy.

To use an analogy, a professional hockey player has the freedom to skate around with pads, a hockey stick, and puck, and do all sorts of maneuvers that most people couldn't hope to accomplish on the spot. He has trained and worked hard for that freedom, and skating and shooting a puck feel natural to him; the stick feels like an extension of his own body. He is not enslaved by any physical barriers to his success because he has diligently worked to grow in physical strength, flexibility, and skill. In a similar manner, people who have true spiritual freedom have that same sense of freedom when trying to choose what is morally good in the face of temptation or pressure to do otherwise. They have trained their souls well so that sin does not enslave them. They've put the time in, and have worked hard, just like the hockey pro who put long hours in an ice rink. It should be noted that although the hockey player exercises his true freedom to excel in the game, he does not have the freedom to change the rules, take his skates off, and throw an extra puck into the rink, because this would seriously wound his relationship with his teammates, his opponents, and his fans and ultimately take away the joy of playing the game. Likewise, spiritual freedom does not give us the license to change moral laws. Rather, it provides the strength of character to be able to follow them.

Whenever we begin to take sin seriously and try to live a moral life, two things will become abundantly clear to us. The first is that we are happier when we don't sin. The second is that it is extremely difficult or even impossible for us to avoid falling into sin again, although we can certainly grow spiritually by the grace of God. So as we strive to follow Christ, we find within ourselves disordered desires, and we'll begin to experience a spiritual tension in our souls. Even though we *want* to do what is right, we find that part of us still desires things that we know aren't good for us or our relationships. Something inside of us is bent toward things that aren't good for us. St. Paul writes about this in his Letter to the Romans: "I do not understand my own actions. For I do not do what I want, but I do the very thing I hate" (7:15, RSVCE). The Church calls this tendency toward sin "concupiscence" (see CCC 405), and acknowledges that it is part of our human condition. We all experience this inclination toward sin and are called to fight against it.

But despite this discord in our souls, we should *never* despair or allow our personal sin to discourage us. There is a huge difference between a healthy recognition of guilt and an experience of shame. A sense of guilt simply means we recognize we did something wrong that hopefully leads us to repentance and taking responsibility for our sin. But shame is when we shut down and hide from God, just as Adam and Eve hid after the first fall, and it is a common tactic of the enemy. Indeed, one wonders what might have happened had Adam and Eve simply owned what they had done and apologized, rather than seeking to blame everyone but themselves!

We should also keep in mind that even the saints sinned, some of them grievously, before their conversion. If someone as holy as the apostle who wrote most of the books in the New Testament *still* struggled with sin, we shouldn't be overly hard on ourselves when we find ourselves doing the same. Instead, we should immediately express sorrow and repentance, and strive eagerly not to fall again.

You may recall the words that Jesus said to St. Faustina, which I shared in the Introduction to this book: "The greater the sinner, the greater the right he has to my Mercy."[12] When we fall, remember the story of the prodigal son. When we acknowledge our sin and return to the Father, He always runs to meet us and welcome us home.

The Sacrament of Reconciliation

Catholics believe that the primary place where repentance and healing happen is the Sacrament of Reconciliation, also called Confession. In Confession we confess our sins out loud to the priest, who, with the authority and power of Christ Himself, forgives us and reconciles us to God and the Church.

The idea of Confession can seem scary or weird to people, but the reality is that it is one of the most beautiful experiences that we can have in this life. The confessional is a place of healing. It is a place of victory and redemption, where chains are broken and we experience the true spiritual freedom for which we were made. Jesus Himself instituted the Sacrament of Confession when He gave His apostles the power to forgive sins:

> On the evening of that day, the first day of the week, the doors being shut where the disciples were, for fear of the Jews, Jesus came and stood among them and said to them, "Peace be with you." When he had said this, he showed them his hands and his side. Then the disciples were glad when they saw the Lord. Jesus said to them again, "Peace be with you. As the Father has sent me, even so I send you."

[12] *The Diary of Saint Maria Faustina Kowalska,* p. 292, entry 723.

> And when he had said this, he breathed on them, and said to them, "Receive the Holy Spirit. If you forgive the sins of any, they are forgiven; if you retain the sins of any, they are retained." (John 20:19–23, RSVCE)

One of the things that I find fascinating about this event is that Jesus gives the apostles the power to forgive sins *when they were in the greatest need of forgiveness themselves*. This story from the Gospel of John takes place on Easter Sunday. All of the apostles, with the exception of John, had run away and abandoned Jesus in His darkest hour. Even Peter, who said he would go to be arrested and even die with Jesus, denied Him three times and fled into the night, weeping bitterly. Now, some of the apostles had witnessed the empty tomb, and many had heard rumors of a resurrection. For a moment, imagine yourself in the shoes of the apostles, wondering what Jesus was going to do or say to them. Would He be upset with them? Would He denounce them and take away the privileges they had as His closest followers because of their cowardice? Jesus does neither of these things. He brings only peace, and breathes the Holy Spirit on them, and gives them the power to forgive sins — a power they passed on to their successors, down to the bishops and priests of today.

Why would Jesus choose to offer forgiveness of sins through men who were themselves sinners? Quite simply: *because we need to hear the words of forgiveness and absolution spoken to us.* Being able to hear the words "You are forgiven," and knowing that these words were first spoken to other sinful people, is transformational and life-giving to the soul. There is a reason that Confession is called a sacrament of *healing*. Though it is difficult, we *can* overcome our struggle with particular sins. Repentant prayer and the Sacrament of Reconciliation are two tools that help us do so.

How to Go to Confession

One of the precepts of the Church is that Catholics receive the Sacrament of Confession at least once a year, but we are encouraged to attend much more frequently, and we especially must go whenever we find ourselves particularly wounded by sin or guilty of a grave or mortal sin (see below). That being said, perhaps it has been far longer since the last time you went. No matter how long it's been, though, *do not be ashamed.* Go and receive this Sacrament as soon as you are able to. Jesus wants you to experience the healing that He has in store for you.

Before going to receive this Sacrament, make an *examination of conscience.* An examination of conscience is a look inward to see where we have sinned, typically based on the Ten Commandments. We've included one in the back of the book (Appendix B) that can serve as a great place to start. You can find more specialized examinations of conscience for different ages and stages of life online at the United States Conference of Catholic Bishops website.[13]

When going to Confession, it is important to hold nothing back. If we are serious about turning from sin, we need to acknowledge what we have done so that God can grant us the grace to avoid sinning again. The Church distinguishes between venial sins, which are everyday faults that we struggle with, and grave sins, which seriously wound our relationship with God, ourselves, or others. When a grave sin is committed with *full knowledge* and *complete consent,* it is considered *mortal,* which means that it completely cuts us off from grace in our soul (CCC 1858–1859). We always need to confess grave sins,

[13] United States Conference of Catholic Bishops, "Examinations of Conscience," accessed November 27, 2024, https://www.usccb.org/prayer-and-worship/sacraments-and-sacramentals/penance/examinations-of-conscience.

and ought to confess venial sins as well. When we do, Jesus, through the words of the priest, brings His healing and mercy.

As you prepare for your Confession, also remember to *not be afraid* of what you will confess. Priests have heard it all before, and they understand how deeply wounded our human nature is. They are sinners too, just like the apostles. Go, confess, and hear the words of absolution spoken out loud so that they can resonate through your ears and into your heart. As Scripture promises us, "If we say we have no sin, we deceive ourselves, and the truth is not in us. If we confess our sins, he is faithful and just, and will forgive our sins and cleanse us from all unrighteousness" (1 John 1:8–9, RSVCE).

✎ Action Step ✎

MAKE A PLAN to receive the Sacrament of Confession. Look up your local parishes' Confession times and schedule it into your calendar. If it's been a while, or if your local parish lists Confessions as "By appointment only," call your parish and set a day and time. As preparation for receiving the Sacrament, be sure to spend some time making an examination of conscience. If you feel like something is holding you back from receiving this Sacrament, or you need space to write out your thoughts or process as you make your examination, feel free to begin journaling about it in the space below. If the Sacrament of Confession is already a regular part of your spiritual life, I encourage you to spend some time here reflecting on how this Sacrament has made an impact on your life and journal about it.

📖 Going Deeper 📖

TONS OF INCREDIBLE books and resources are available about the Sacrament of Confession and why it is important. Here is a short list to help you get started if you are still struggling to understand it or simply want to learn more:

- ✠ *Lord, Have Mercy: The Healing Power of Confession* by Scott Hahn
- ✠ *7 Secrets of Confession* by Vinny Flynn
- ✠ *Pocket Guide to the Sacrament of Reconciliation* by Fr. Mike Schmitz and Fr. Josh Johnson
- ✠ *Forgiven: The Transforming Power of Confession* — Video series by the Augustine Institute

Day 5

Receiving Holy Communion

Putting reception of the Eucharist so close to the start may seem strange for a book about Christian prayer, but the reality is that everything we could ever hope to receive from God is present to us here under the disguise of simple bread and wine. The Eucharist is the "source and summit" of our faith as Christians (CCC 1324): "Unless you eat the flesh of the Son of man and drink his blood, you have no life in you" (John 6:53, RSVCE); "The cup of blessing that we bless, is it not a participation in the blood of Christ? The bread that we break, is it not a participation in the body of Christ?" (1 Cor. 10:16–17, NABRE). It truly is the greatest gift, the "abundance of life" that Jesus promised to give us (see John 10:10). Though it still looks and tastes like bread and wine, it is Jesus. When we receive the Eucharist, we are becoming one with Jesus — which is really the whole point of the spiritual life, the summit to which we all are striving.

Unfortunately, the Eucharist is misunderstood not only in our relationship with other Christian denominations but even within the Church. Recent surveys have shown that a significant percentage of Catholics don't believe in the true presence of Jesus in the Eucharist, and as many as half aren't sure or are incorrect about what the Church's actual teaching is.[14]

[14] Pew Research Center, "What Americans Know about Religion," July 23, 2019, https://www.pewresearch.org/religion/2019/07/23/what-americans-know-about-religion/.

Put simply, the Eucharist is Jesus: His Body, Blood, Soul, and Divinity. When we receive the Eucharist, we receive Jesus. As we saw in the words of Scripture above, Jesus tells us in His own words He came so that we might have abundant life, that His flesh is true food and His blood is true drink, and that unless we eat His flesh and drink His blood we don't have life within us. Then, at the Last Supper, He told the apostles that the bread and wine are His body and blood and commanded them to continue offering the Eucharist in perpetuity — "Do this in remembrance of me" (Luke 22:19, RSVCE).

Jesus wants us to receive the Eucharist because He wants us to have *His* life within *us*. The Word became flesh in the Incarnation. The Word becomes food in the Eucharist.

The Catholic Liturgy

Though we can receive Communion by having it brought to us at home or while at work (especially in places like hospitals or nursing homes when people are unable to travel to church), the most fitting place to receive Holy Communion is within the Church's liturgical celebration, called the Mass in the Roman Catholic Church or Divine Liturgy in the Eastern Catholic Churches.

When we receive the Eucharist with open hearts and a desire to receive everything He wants to give us, we become more like Jesus. We have all heard at one point or another the age-old maxim "You are what you eat," and the Eucharist is the spiritual food from heaven that makes us more and more like Jesus. For example, look at St. Catherine of Siena, who consumed the Eucharist as her only source of food for seven years. During that time, she authored countless letters and spiritual writings, convinced the Pope to move back to Rome (effectively ending a decades-long schism), experienced mystical visions, and transformed the lives of those around her, including the sick and poor. All she ate was Jesus, and in doing so allowed Him to shine through her in a powerful way.

Unfortunately, many people's experience of receiving the Eucharist is far from extraordinary. Countless people receive the Eucharist totally unaware of the reality that is being offered to them, and others who have been told their whole lives about the Eucharist don't feel like they really get anything spiritually from it. But the power of the Eucharist is completely separate from how the faithful *feel* after receiving it. While some of us may experience the grace of comfort, peace, joy, or other emotions after receiving the Eucharist, its real power is beyond human comprehension or feeling. In the end, when you receive Jesus in the form of bread or wine, you have His life within you. You become a living tabernacle of the Word Incarnate. You unite yourself with Christ, His Church, and His mission. This is the true power of the Eucharist.

From yet another perspective, many people look at things like the many scandals that have rocked the Church and ask themselves how something like this could happen with people who are receiving the Eucharist every single day. St. Paul has some words that apply here:

> Whoever, therefore, eats the bread or drinks the cup of the Lord in an unworthy manner will be guilty of profaning the body and blood of the Lord. Let a man examine himself, and so eat of the bread and drink of the cup. For anyone who eats and drinks without discerning the body eats and drinks judgment upon himself. (1 Cor. 11:27–29, RSVCE)

This passage helps explain some of the extreme examples. It's clear from St. Paul's words that receiving Communion with a total unbelief or any sort of serious unrepented sin can actually do damage to our souls, instead of being the healing balm that the Eucharist is meant to be. Without repentance and turning away from sin, there is no room for the grace of the Eucharist to penetrate our heart and transform us.

Another problem that I think is really common in the Church today is that people simply aren't receiving the Eucharist *enough*. In most parishes, at least in the United States, only about 24 percent of the parishioners will be in attendance on a given weekend.[15] A significant number will only be at Mass on Christmas, Ash Wednesday, and Easter. But we have to understand that the Eucharist is not a one-and-done cure; it's more like a *prescription medication*. When a patient goes to a doctor to get treatment for a disease, the treatment usually consists of medicine that needs to be taken over a series of days. When we miss a dose, the treatment loses its effectiveness, or if we only take it once or twice and forget to follow the directions, it can totally jeopardize the whole treatment plan and even make the pathogen more resistant to the medication. The Eucharist is God's prescription for sin and brokenness in our lives and our hearts.

In addition, you can take certain actions before receiving Communion that can aid you in experiencing its power. The first is to maintain a relationship with God through a daily prayer life. (Since you are reading this book, you are off to a great start already!) Grace builds upon nature, and the deeper your relationship is with the Lord, the more intimate your experience of Holy Communion will be. Scripture often uses the image of a bride and a groom to represent the relationship with God and His people, and just as deeper love between spouses facilitates a deeper experience of intimacy when they come together, a deeper love between the soul and God will lead to a deeper sense of intimacy when that soul is united with Him in Holy Communion.

[15] CARA (Center for Applied Research in the Apostolate), "Frequently Requested Church Statistics," accessed November 27, 2024, https://cara.georgetown.edu/faqs.

We should also have certain interior spiritual dispositions when receiving Communion. The most important is to know that you are in a state of grace, with no mortal sins weighing on your soul, which is why it is important to go to Confession regularly. You should also be open to whatever the Lord wants to do in your heart. A mental prayer along the lines of giving permission for the Lord to work in your heart and heal what needs to be healed is a powerful way to start.

Action Step

For your action step today, make a plan to attend Mass and receive Communion one more day this week than you typically do. If you haven't been in a long time, go on Sunday. If you go every week, add a weekday Mass to your schedule. Daily Masses are typically much shorter than Sunday Masses! Look at the parish websites in your area and try to find a time that works with your schedule. To help hold yourself accountable, write here the times that you will attend and add them to your calendar.

🕮 Going Deeper 🕮

HERE ARE SOME notable books about the Eucharist that can help you grow in devotion to this beautiful Sacrament:

- ✠ *Jesus, Our Eucharistic Love* by Fr. Stefano M. Manelli, F. I.
- ✠ *Eucharist* by Bishop Robert Barron
- ✠ *The Lamb's Supper* by Scott Hahn
- ✠ *Consuming the Word* by Scott Hahn
- ✠ *7 Secrets of the Eucharist* by Vinny Flynn
- ✠ *Jesus and the Jewish Roots of the Eucharist* by Brant Pitre
- ✠ *The Basic Book of the Eucharist* by Lawrence Lovasik
- ✠ *33 Days to Eucharistic Glory* by Matthew Kelly
- ✠ *The Eucharist Is Really Jesus* by Joe Heschmeyer
- ✠ *Presence: The Mystery of the Eucharist* — Video series by the Augustine Institute

Day 6

Reading Scripture

SCRIPTURE IS THE living Word of God. In Christ, the Word became Flesh. In the Eucharist, the Word becomes the Bread of life. In Scripture, the Word became a written revelation of who God is — a book we call the Bible. In later chapters we explore different ways of praying with Scripture. Here we simply take a look at what the Bible is and how to get started with it.

The Church has always taught that the Bible is God's word. It is one of the primary ways that God reveals Himself to humanity. Though God is the primary author of Scripture, He inspired *human* authors to write the actual words, making "full use of their own faculties and powers" so that they are true authors as well.[16] For example, the first five books of the Bible are traditionally attributed to Moses, King David is regarded to have written many of the psalms, and St. Paul wrote much of the New Testament. Throughout this whole process, the Holy Spirit guided each author, keeping him from error and ensuring that God's full message would be communicated in writing. Yet at no point did God dictate the Bible word for word to the human authors, whose personalities, cultures, and individual

[16] Vatican Council II, Dogmatic Constitution on Divine Revelation *Dei verbum* (November 18, 1965), https://www.vatican.va/archive/hist_councils/ii_vatican_council/documents/vat-ii_const_19651118_dei-verbum_en.html, no. 11.

backgrounds clearly shine through even as the Holy Spirit inspired each story, message, and phrase.

The Bible consists of two sections, the Old Testament and the New Testament, and both together tell the story of mankind's redemption. In the Old Testament, we read of our Creation, our Fall, and the promises of our redemption. In the beginning of the Scripture, we find that we were made in God's image and likeness. We enjoyed intimacy and authentic communion with God, but we fell into sin. The effects of that first Fall echoed across the cosmos and wounded the relationship between God and man. The human race was cut off from divine life, unable to contain it because of the brokenness of our relationship with God.

However, that wasn't the end of the story. Throughout the ages God began to call certain individuals to Himself, building up a small family into a nation and eventually a kingdom and dynasty. Though the kingdom fell into ruin and was taken into captivity, He continued to speak to His people through prophets, and began to foretell a day when they would be redeemed and their sins would be blotted away forever. A messiah would come and redeem Israel, restoring it to a greater glory than it had ever had and setting it free from oppression. Not only that, but a "suffering servant" would come and take on all of the weight of the sin of the world and abolish it (see Isa. 52:13–53:12).

From there we head into the New Testament, which tells the story of Jesus, the carpenter from Nazareth. He came to redeem not only Israel but the whole human race, and He did it by freely taking on all the sin of the world — past, present, and future — and put sin to death in Himself on the Cross. He was Emmanuel, God with us, for He was both the Son of God and the son of Mary. He is fully divine, yet fully human. He is *both* the long-awaited Messiah who was foretold by the prophets *as well as* the suffering servant who wiped away the sins of the world by taking them onto Himself and destroying them.

Also in the New Testament, we read about how Jesus established His Church, and we are told how to live as followers of Christ as we get a clearer sense of who God is. Finally, at the end of the Bible we see how we are destined to live in God's kingdom forever. We learn that Christ began the process of Redemption when He carried out His mission two thousand years ago, but His kingdom is still manifesting itself in time and space. At the end of time there will be a "new creation" where we, and all of the created world, will be made new. There will be no more sorrow or tears, and we will see God — the source of all Beauty, Truth, and Goodness — face-to-face as He is, in all His fullness.

Put in its most simple expression, the Bible is God's love story to you and me. It is a place where His Heart speaks to our hearts. The Bible teaches us just how far God is willing to go to redeem us, and it shows us the vast expanse of His great love for us. To listen, we must read not only with eyes but with our hearts.

How to Read the Bible

Though the Bible has one vast overarching story, it really is a collection of books, seventy-three of them to be exact. There are all sorts of genres: mythic literature, poetry, books of law and liturgical practice, songs, prophetic writings, biographical accounts, and more. Some books have simple and straightforward narratives, and others can be more confusing.

When beginning to read the Bible for the first time, many people start it like they would any other book — at the beginning. Although this may seem natural, it's generally recommended that people begin by reading the New Testament. I recommend beginning with one of the Gospels. The Gospels are the first four books of the New Testament, and they tell who Jesus was and offer an account of His public ministry. From there, I recommend reading the Acts of the Apostles, which reveals everything that happened immediately after Jesus ascended into heaven. Next, read Romans and James. Although all of the New Testament letters are also great to read for beginners, these two are particularly beneficial for those new to reading the Bible. After that, go back and read the books that present the main plot of the Old Testament leading up to Jesus' arrival: Genesis, Exodus, Numbers, Joshua, Judges, 1 and 2 Samuel, 1 and 2 Kings, Ezra, Nehemiah, and 1 Maccabees. These books will give you a firm handle on the big picture of salvation history. After you read all that, I simply recommend asking the Holy Spirit to lead you to different books and check them off your list as you go.

When you are reading the Bible, the most important thing to do is remember that you are praying. Start with the sign of the Cross, and invite the Holy Spirit to guide you. When something strikes you or moves your heart in a particular way, put the Bible down and sit with it for a little bit. Allow God's peaceful presence to fill you—and take time to soak it in. It helps to keep in mind that prayer consists of four primary movements — talking to God, listening to God, thinking about God, and being with God. Find ways to incorporate each of these as you read, writing down in a prayer journal thoughts that strike you and questions that arise.

When it comes to reading Scripture, you get better with practice. Opening the Bible, especially if it's been awhile, is often the hardest step. There are other chapters with different techniques for praying with Scripture ahead, but for now — simply begin.

✎ Action Step ✎

YOUR ACTION STEP today is to dive into Scripture! Spend ten to fifteen minutes with the Bible open in front of you. You don't have to be reading the whole time. In fact, I encourage you to pause often and write down things that jump out at you. Talk to God about them or write about them in your prayer journal or the space below. Also, when you are done, put your Bible in a visible place so that you are reminded to pick it up from time to time in the future as well!

Going Deeper

FANTASTIC BOOKS ON Scripture are almost impossible to contain to a short list. Here are two of my favorites that have been wonderful in helping me understand the Bible more deeply:

- *Bible Basics for Catholics: A New Picture of Salvation History* by John Bergsma
- *A Father Who Keeps His Promises* by Scott Hahn

There is also an incredible podcast called *The Bible in a Year* by Fr. Mike Schmitz. He presents the Bible as 365 manageable chunks that you can listen to throughout the course of a year. In addition to reading the passages, Fr. Mike briefly explains what is taking place. It's certainly worth checking out.

In addition to books and resources about the Bible, there are also many wonderful Bibles out there with resources already included that help you learn how to navigate Scripture and learn more about God's Word. For those who are looking to understand the big picture of the Bible better, I recommend the *Great Adventure Bible* by Ascension Press. For those who have lots of big questions that arise as they read and like getting into the nitty-gritty, the *Ignatius Catholic Study Bible* with commentary by Scott Hahn and Curtis Mitch has incredible line-by-line footnotes that help you understand the context and depth of the text. At the end of the day, the best Bible you can have is the one that you read, so don't get too caught up on wondering if you have a certain version. Just start reading and you'll learn more as you go along!

Day 7

Prayer and Fasting

THE TWO DAYS on which Catholics are required to fast are Ash Wednesday and Good Friday. On these two days we only are allowed one full meal and two small meals that together equal no more than a full meal. No snacking is allowed.[17] On Fridays during Lent we are also to abstain from meat (which is why we see local fish fries and Filet O'Fish commercials pop up around this time of year). Though it isn't as well known, Catholics are also required to make a similar sacrifice every Friday throughout the entire year — either abstaining from meat or making an equal act of sacrifice — to commemorate and unite ourselves to Jesus' death, which took place on a Friday, just as every Sunday is a commemoration of Jesus' Resurrection in a special way.[18]

17 This requirement applies to all Catholics ages eighteen to fifty-nine who do not have any health issues that would prevent them from fasting. See United States Conference of Catholic Bishops, "Fast & Abstinence," accessed November 27, 2024, https://www.usccb.org/prayer-and-worship/liturgical-year-and-calendar/lent/catholic-information-on-lenten-fast-and-abstinence.

18 Fridays that fall on Solemnities or major feast days are typically exempt from these rules. See National Conference of Catholic Bishops, "Pastoral Statement on Penance and Abstinence," November 18, 1966, https://www.usccb.org/prayer-and-worship/liturgical-year-and-calendar/lent/us-bishops-pastoral-statement-on-penance-and-abstinence, article 16.

Though fasting most commonly involves food, we can also fast from other things or find other small but meaningful sacrifices. For example, we might give up social media or video games for a few days, or replace our usual car ride playlist or podcast with something prayerful. One creative example I recently learned was to simply turn the color off of a smartphone to make it black-and-white and less attractive to spend time on. There really are countless ways to incorporate this discipline into your spiritual life.

Why Do We Fast?

The reason that followers of Jesus fast has several layers. As we begin to peel them back, we find that, at its core, fasting is first and foremost meant to be an *experience of prayer*. Fasting is meant to draw us out of worldly concerns and into deeper awareness of the presence of God in our life. There are other aspects and benefits as well — for example, it helps us both to grow in self-discipline and to orient our will (the part of our soul that desires things) toward God instead of worldliness. Also, when we fast we are imitating Jesus, who spent much of His time on earth in prayer and fasting. Fasting is *not* a diet. It is as much a spiritual experience as a bodily one, maybe even more so. If we focus purely on what we are giving up, without taking time to fill ourselves with God through prayer, we are not fasting.

A certain *spiritual power* is also present in fasting. In Matthew's Gospel, after the Transfiguration, we find Jesus with Peter, James, and John coming down from the mountain to find a young boy possessed with a stubborn demon that had refused to be cast out — even by some of Jesus' own disciples who had experience in that area. With a few words, Jesus commands the demon to leave, and in an instant He cures the boy. When the disciples come to Him asking why they could not cast out the demon, Jesus mentions both their lack of faith and that this particular kind of spirit can only come out by prayer and *fasting* (Mark 9:14–29).

When referring to the spiritual power of fasting, St. Augustine wrote, "Fasting cleanses the soul, raises the mind, subjects one's flesh to the spirit, renders the heart contrite and humble, scatters the clouds of concupiscence, quenches the fire of lust, and kindles the true light of chastity. Enter again into yourself."[19] Pay special attention to the last line of this quotation. When we fast, we grow in temperance and self-control. When we grow in this way, we experience the freedom to be our authentic selves, a task that is difficult when we are wrestling with concupiscence. When we are fully in control of ourselves, we are in a very real sense experiencing the deep spiritual freedom that we reflected on a couple days ago. Fasting is a tool we can use to subdue our passions and sinful inclinations. In fact, whenever we find ourselves struggling with a particular habitual sin or vice that we can't seem to kick, incorporating some kind of fasting into our prayer and the daily routine of our lives may be exactly what we need to finally break free.

And so we must remember that at the heart of our fast is the call to *self-gift*, especially regarding our relationship with God, but also other human relationships. If we want to give ourselves fully to another, such as our spouse or family or simply to authentic service in charity, we need to be fully in control of our desires. Conversion begins in the heart or mind, but at some point it needs to make its way into the will as well. Not only should we strive to know and love God more, we should also strive to *want what He wants for us*. There is no greater tool for self-surrender to God's will than through the prayerful incorporation of fasting.

[19] Augustine, *On Prayer and Fasting* (De orat. et Jejun. [Serm. lxxii (ccxxx, de Tempore)]).

Finally, because fasting is a form of sacrifice it also can become a participation in Jesus' sacrifice on the Cross. "Now I rejoice in my sufferings for your sake, and in my flesh I complete what is lacking in Christ's afflictions for the sake of his body, that is, the church" (Col. 1:24, RSVCE). What St. Paul is speaking about here is the idea of *redemptive suffering*. In other words, because we are members of Christ's Body, we have the opportunity to participate in His self-offering on the Cross. We can unite our sufferings (and sacrifices) to His own for building up the Church, even participating in some mysterious way in His redemptive plan for humanity. This doesn't take away from Jesus' sacrifice or role as the one mediator between God and mankind. Rather, it shows the wonderful mercy and love of a Creator who allows His creation to participate in His work. Though we won't know exactly how until the day we see God face-to-face, we can be assured that our sacrifices and fasts make a difference in God's plan of redemption.

Dangers to Avoid

There are many spiritual benefits to incorporating fasting into your life, but we also need to be aware of some common pitfalls in order to avoid them. At the root of all of them is a lack of focus on Jesus. For example, we can become too legalistic — focusing too much on the fast itself, becoming anxious if we forget some aspect of it or wondering if we are doing enough. It's one thing to reflect about something; it's another to stress about it. If you struggle with scrupulosity or anxiety, always remember that God wants you to feel fully alive. First and foremost, God desires the peace of His presence to reign in your heart.

Another pitfall is focusing too much on ourselves. One example of this is when we come into Lent with a focus on self-improvement rather than on drawing closer to God. Even though self-improvement often comes about as a direct result of being closer to God, it's worth asking ourselves what our true purpose is. If health or simply the rush of doing something challenging is the main focus of our fast, we are missing the point.

I also want to recognize fasting in light of the fact that we are facing a mental health crisis in the United States, especially among young people. Anxiety, depression, eating disorders, and the like are sadly an all-too-common struggle and burden. While none of these define a person — our deepest identity is always as a son or daughter of God — if we struggle in one of these ways, and especially if we struggle with body image or eating disorders, we need to exercise prudence in regard to food-related fasting. If you are ever unsure, consider talking to a mental health professional who also has a background and understanding of the Christian spiritual Tradition, or talk with a spiritual director or someone you look up to as a spiritual role model to help you grow. Consider finding non-food-related fasts.

As a final note, Catholics are also required to fast for at least one hour before receiving Communion. This helps us be more attentive and approach the Sacrament spiritually hungry. Remember, the only required fasts from the Church are Good Friday and Ash Wednesday and the fast before receiving Holy Communion. In addition, we abstain from meat on Fridays of Lent and make a similar sacrifice on Fridays throughout the rest of the year. Everything else, even the practice of giving things up for Lent, are personal decisions between you and God. That being said, everyone who wants to follow Jesus more closely should strive to incorporate this important spiritual practice into their life.

✎ Action Item ✎

TAKE A FEW minutes to create a fasting plan, beginning with Fridays. Traditionally, Catholics gave up meat every Friday throughout the year, but in the United States we are allowed to substitute this sacrifice for something else. Perhaps you could give up sweets or social media. If you are currently in the Lenten season and already giving something up, great! Even so, consider adding one more small sacrifice to the rest of the liturgical season, perhaps only on Fridays. Write your game plan below or in your journal, and set reminders for yourself so you don't forget.

Going Deeper

IF YOU WANT to learn more about prayer and abstinence, you can also check out the papal encyclical *Paenitimini* ("On Fast and Abstinence") by Pope Paul VI. There are also many wonderful Scripture passages about fasting that you can sit and contemplate. You'll find a handful of them below.

- ✠ Joel 2:12
- ✠ Exodus 34:28
- ✠ Luke 4:1–4
- ✠ Jonah 3:5–10

Each of these passages reveals a slightly different lens on fasting, and I encourage you to read them and sit with them a bit. Write down any thoughts and questions that you have.

Day 8

Prayer in Community

When the early Church was just getting started, "They devoted themselves to the apostles' teaching and fellowship, to the breaking of bread and prayers" (Acts 2:42, RSVCE).

In the early days of the Church, following Christ was not simply a matter of personal faith. The early Church committed themselves to fellowship with one another, adhered to the teachings of the Apostles, and frequently received the Eucharist. They addressed each other as brother and sister, and St. Paul directed them through his letters how to live with one another in community.

Jesus Himself told us that the definitive characteristic that will reveal His disciples to the world is the *love that they will have for one another*, and this love must mirror the love that He has for us (John 13:34–35). Then, at the Last Supper, Jesus prayed that all of His followers "might be one" as He and the Father "are one." As Jesus' disciples, we are ultimately called to authentic communion with one another through the Eucharist and through our love for one another.

As we move into the days ahead, we'll be looking at many of the different religious orders and Christian spiritual movements that have formed over the past millennia. Each of these movements has at least two things in common: a devotion to Christ and a call to community. The Church has always placed an emphasis on community because mankind was made for community. One of the central truths to the biblical Creation account is that "it is not good that the man should be alone" (Gen. 2:18, RSVCE). We were made for God, and God is a *communion* of Persons. The goal of the Christian life is to enter into the Divine Community and bring as many people as possible with us. No man is an island. No one can walk the Christian life alone.

However, there can be no authentic community without true vulnerability. To be vulnerable means to open yourself to the possibility of being wounded by someone, but trusting them so much that you know they will not take advantage of this privilege. In order to grow in community, we need to learn to be vulnerable — first with ourselves and with God, and then with others. Heaven itself is often described as the perfect community — where we are fully united with God and one another. This means there is also a certain level of vulnerability in heaven, though it would be a vulnerability that has no fear.

Finally, community also plays an important role in encouraging and building one another up. Our spiritual brothers and sisters inspire us and help us as accountability partners as we journey together toward Christ. Members of a community pray for each other and push each other to grow closer to Jesus. They support one another in difficult times and celebrate the good times. They model the love of God to each other and to the world (see John 13:35).

Action Item

TAKE SOME TIME to reflect on your own personal parish faith community. Do you feel like you are being called to participate more deeply in the life of your parish in any way? Do you have people you can talk to about faith — perhaps even an accountability partner or small group that you are going through this book with? Write down below some ways that you think you are being called deeper into community, and then take some time to pray for your community. If finding community has been a struggle for you, take time to intentionally pray and ask God to help you find someplace where community is a reality.

____

____

____

____

Going Deeper

IF YOU WANT to learn more about the importance of community or how to practically build spiritual community into the daily structure of your life, I highly recommend the book *Called to Community: The Life Jesus Wants for His People* (edited by Charles E. Moore). It's composed of brief writings about the importance of community from many Christian saints and spiritual writers throughout history, such as St. Benedict of Nursia, Søren Kierkegaard, Dietrich Bonhoeffer, Mother Teresa, C. S. Lewis, and Thomas Merton.

Day 9

Prayer in Action (The Works of Mercy)

WHEN WE BEGIN to take time for prayer seriously, it overflows into every aspect of our life. We begin to see things not from our own perspective but from God's. We grow in wisdom and peacefulness, and are filled with the other gifts and fruits of the Holy Spirit. In other words, God begins to transform us from the inside out. His presence fills us and overflows in us. We experience exactly what Jesus tells us in Scripture, the "living water" flowing into and out from our hearts. Oftentimes, this means that prayer *leads us to action.*

The end of our designated prayer time does not necessarily mean the end of our prayer. In fact, one of the goals of designated prayer time is to help us pray throughout the rest of the day. St. Paul tells us in Scripture to "pray without ceasing" (1 Thess. 5:17, NABRE). Our whole life can be prayer, especially when we are actively seeking to help others — to be the hands and feet of Christ in a broken world that needs Him.

In the Gospels, Jesus tells us that when we "feed the hungry," "clothe the naked," and "visit the imprisoned," we are truly feeding, clothing, and visiting Him. As we grow closer to God, we begin to see His face in the faces of everyone we see, especially those who find themselves in need in one way or another. In prayer we are filled with Jesus' presence; in prayer we then bring that presence to others. The examples above are just three of what we call the Corporal Works of Mercy. The Corporal Works of Mercy all revolve around meeting people's most basic necessities, recognizing the face of Jesus in all of God's people, and in a very real way *bringing* Jesus to them by ministering to them. There are seven of them altogether:

- ✠ Feed the hungry.
- ✠ Give drink to the thirsty.
- ✠ Shelter the homeless.
- ✠ Visit the sick.
- ✠ Visit the imprisoned.
- ✠ Bury the dead.
- ✠ Give alms to the poor.

Along with these, we also have seven Spiritual Works of Mercy, which are also a long-standing part of our Christian heritage and find their roots in Jesus' actions while He walked among us. As Christians we recognize that there are both physical and spiritual needs that people have, and so we should strive to meet both sets of needs. The Spiritual Works of Mercy are to

- ✠ Counsel the doubtful.
- ✠ Instruct the ignorant.
- ✠ Admonish the sinner.
- ✠ Comfort the sorrowful.
- ✠ Forgive injuries.
- ✠ Bear wrongs patiently.

- ✠ Pray for the living and the dead.

There is an intimate connection between prayer and charity. In fact, Scripture tells us that without good works (meaning these sorts of Corporal and Spiritual Works of Mercy), our faith is *dead* (see James 2:14–26). These are strong words—and quite convicting. When we meet Jesus face-to-face, He's going to ask us to give an account for how well we loved others. Let's roll up our sleeves and get to work!

Action Step

TAKE TIME TO look over the lists of Corporal and Spiritual Works of Mercy. Just as different methods and styles of prayer speak more deeply to certain people, each of us has a unique role to play in building God's kingdom and serving others. Which of these works do you feel God is calling you to do more? What are some ways that you can carry out this Work of Mercy in the world? Make an action plan to start. It can be something you commit to weekly, monthly, or even simply seasonally. Donating old clothes, serving in a soup kitchen, getting involved in a parish ministry, visiting a relative in a nursing home — these are just a handful of countless examples. Don't try to do everything all at once. Rather, pick one or two works of mercy and a reasonable time frame and make it happen. Not only will it bless the people you are serving, it will bring greater joy to your heart as well — it is still prayer, after all!

Make a plan and write it out in the space below. Mark your calendar and begin setting things in motion to make it happen. Be specific: if your plan calls for it, call an organization like a soup kitchen or food pantry to schedule a time to visit and help.

Going Deeper

THE UNITED STATES Conference of Catholic Bishops has wonderful guides to both the Corporal and Spiritual Works of Mercy. You can find them at USCCB.org by typing "Works of Mercy" in the search bar.

Day 10

Finding God in Silence

JUST AS WE can experience God through the gift of music, we can also encounter Him in silence. Music is the height of vocal prayer, but silence is the beginning of meditation and learning to listen. Praying in silence means not only that we are quiet exteriorly with our voices; we make room for interior silence as well. We push aside all distracting thoughts and simply acknowledge that God is present. Many monks and sisters from various religious orders work silence into their routine in some fashion.

Silence is absolutely crucial in Christian prayer, having its roots in Sacred Scripture. When the prophet Elijah fled into the wilderness to escape those who sought to take his life, God revealed Himself in a very particular way:

> And behold, the LORD passed by, and a great and strong wind rent the mountains, and broke in pieces the rocks before the LORD, but the LORD was not in the wind; and after the wind an earthquake, but the LORD was not in the earthquake; and after the earthquake a fire, but the LORD was not in the fire; and after the fire a still small voice. And when Eli′jah heard it, he wrapped his face in his mantle and went out and stood at the entrance of the cave. And behold, there came a voice to him, and said, "What are you doing here, Eli′jah?" (1 Kgs. 19:11–13, RSVCE)

God did not reveal Himself to Elijah in a great and powerful manner such as the great pillar of fire or column of smoke that led the Israelites through the wilderness. It was not with a thundering voice that God chose to speak with him. Rather, God revealed Himself to be a "still small voice," one that would have been easily missed if Elijah was not listening for it.

In the New Testament, we see the importance of silence that Jesus modeled for us. The Gospels are filled with moments that show Jesus stepping away from the noise of the crowd to go pray (see Matt. 14:23, Mark 6:46–47, and Luke 6:12). Jesus made silent time with His Father a priority, and we need to do the same if we want to be able to hear His voice.

When we make time for silence and intentionally try to hear God's voice, we often find that He wants to bring something to our attention. Usually a certain person or situation or memory comes to mind. Sometimes this can be uncomfortable, but God knows that in order to heal our spiritual and emotional wounds, He often has to bring them to the surface.

Entering into silence takes courage. In silence we have to face the reality of how we stand before ourselves and before God. When we achieve silence exteriorly and interiorly, there is no place for us to hide. We stand naked and exposed before our Creator, and we bring into the light all of our wounds and all of the lies we've believed about ourselves and others so that we can begin to hear God's still small voice of truth and healing.

Sometimes, before entering into this place of interior silence, it helps to simply ask the Lord, "Jesus, what do you want to heal in me today?" — and then wait for Him to speak.

✎ Action Step ✎

YOUR ACTION STEP today is to spend ten minutes in exterior and interior silence. Silence your phone, or even turn it off completely — the psychological effect of this can be incredibly freeing. Try to push aside distractions. If it helps, you can repeat a prayer such as, "Come, Holy Spirit," or "Come, Lord Jesus," to help you clear your mind and help your heart enter. As you approach the point of interior silence, ask the Lord the question I posed above: "Lord, what do you want to heal in me today?" Use the space below to write out what you experienced and what you think the Lord is trying to speak into your life at this time.

____

____

____

____

Going Deeper

IF YOU WANT to learn more about the importance of silence and find ways to cultivate more of it in your life, I recommend the books *The Power of Silence: Against the Dictatorship of Noise* by Cardinal Robert Sarah and *The Hidden Power of Silence in the Mass: A Guide for Encountering Christ in the Liturgy* by Fr. Boniface Hicks, O. S. B.

PART 3

Sacred and Traditional Methods of Prayer

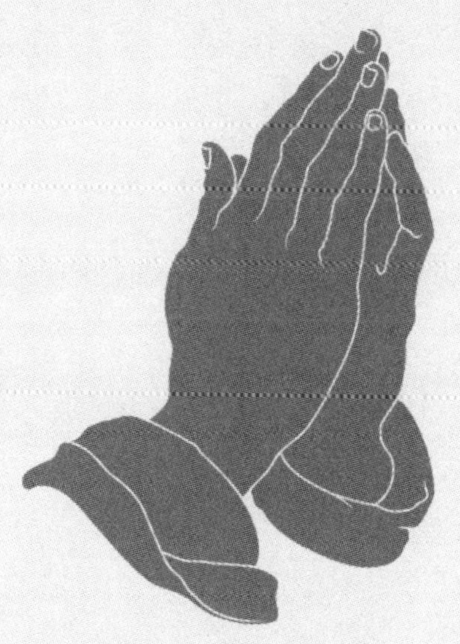

Over the next couple of days, we'll be looking at several traditional methods for prayer that have existed since the earliest centuries of the Church's history. Each of these prayer techniques either began in monastic communities or were formalized by them, before being adopted by the broader Church. They are now integral to the life of the Church. Praying the Liturgy of the Hours is strictly required for all members of the clergy, and the process of *lectio divina* as a way of praying with Scripture has become one of the most well-known Catholic prayer techniques. In the Hours, we join our prayer to the prayer of the Church. In lectio, we are trained in hearing God's voice through the written Word. As you pray through these next two days, keep in mind that you are participating in traditions that go back centuries. My hope is that these beautiful prayer methods nourish your soul and bring you God's peace.

Day 11

The Liturgy of the Hours

IN THE MEDIEVAL Church, it was common for monks and Catholic communities to hold organized communal prayer at different "hours," or scheduled times throughout the day. The idea was that by setting aside certain times for prayer throughout the day, one sanctifies the whole day. As St. Paul writes in Scripture, we should strive to "pray at all times" (Eph. 6:18, RSVCE). Praying at structured times throughout the day is needed to accomplish this noble goal. These prayers became known as the "Divine Office" or the "Liturgy of the Hours." The term "hour" doesn't mean that each prayer segment should take an hour, but rather that traditionally these communal gatherings started at the beginning of an hour. The prayer at each hour can take as little as two minutes or as long as twenty minutes. Over time, this practice of praying at set hours was adopted by the entire Church, and all priests and deacons are required to pray these hours daily as part of their priestly office. Since Vatican II, the Church has also strongly encouraged laypeople and parishes to pray the hours both publicly and privately. There are a total of six different "hours" when we pray the Divine Office.

Every hour in the Liturgy of the Hours involves praying with the psalms. Before and after each psalm segment, an *antiphon* is prayed to help one focus while meditating on the text. There is also often a brief prayer said at the end of the psalm. When praying with a group, usually the leader reads the antiphon at the start of the psalm, then half the group recites the first stanza and the other half recites the second stanza — and so on. At the end, the leader recites the prayer, and the whole group recites the antiphon together. Depending on the Hour, the psalm is then followed by other readings from Scripture and the Church Fathers, prayers of petition and praise, and an examination of conscience.

The hours that we pray at are as follows:

- ✠ **The Invitatory** — The very first moment of the day, typically before sunrise but appropriately said right after waking up. We begin with the prayer "Lord, open my lips. And my mouth shall proclaim your praise." Traditionally, Psalm 95 is then prayed along with a seasonal antiphon, although a handful of other psalms can be used in its place. The Invitatory is the shortest of the different hours that we pray.

- ✠ **Morning and Evening Prayer** — The Second Vatican Council called these the two "hinges" of the Liturgy of the Hours.[20] Each has some introductory prayers, a hymn, three psalms (or other brief poetic sections from Scripture), a reading from the Bible, intercessory prayers and petitions, and an Our Father. They also each contain a canticle from the Gospel of Luke along with an antiphon. In Morning Prayer we pray Zechariah's prayer of thanksgiving upon the birth of John the Baptist, and in Evening Prayer we pray the Magnificat of the Blessed Mother, which she recites when greeted by Elizabeth at the Visitation.

20 Vatican Council II, The Constitution on the Sacred Liturgy *Sacrosanctum concilium* (December 4, 1963), https://www.vatican.va/archive/hist_councils/ii_vatican_council/documents/vat-ii_const_19631204_sacrosanctum-concilium_en.html, no. 89.

- ✠ **The Office of Readings** — This hour also contains a hymn and three psalms or canticles, but they are typically much shorter than the ones from Morning and Evening Prayer. Following these, there are two readings — one from the Bible and one from the commentary of a saint or magisterial document. This can be prayed at any point of the day.
- ✠ **Daytime Prayer** — Traditionally this consisted of three separate hours: midmorning, midday, and midafternoon, and the time of day one chooses to pray determines which hymns and reading are chosen. However, priests and religious are only asked to do one of these. Daytime Prayer is much shorter than the other hours, with the exception of the Invitatory, and consists of a hymn, two short psalm segments, and a brief reading.
- ✠ **Night Prayer** — Said at the very end of the day before going to sleep. After the Introductory prayers, people are encouraged to take time to make an examination of conscience before the hymn. There is one psalm, a brief reading, a responsory prayer, and another canticle from the Gospel of Luke (the prayer of Simeon at the Presentation).

When seeing all of this, your first thought might be, *Whoa! That's a lot of prayer!* You would be right! Altogether, it takes about an hour to pray all six of the hours if you added them all together. And to be clear, for the average layperson there is no set expectation for us to pray all of these every day.

That being said, the Liturgy of the Hours is a beautiful way to sanctify the whole day and, as a result, our whole life. It is *liturgical* prayer, which means that, like the Mass, it is the public prayer of the Church to God. In fact, it is second only to the Mass in being the highest form of prayer that the Church offers to God. While learning to pray the Liturgy of the Hours can be difficult, it is also incredibly rewarding, especially since when we pray these hours, our prayer becomes one with that of the whole Church. Even if we can't pray the Liturgy of the Hours every day, we will still benefit from becoming familiar with it and praying even just parts of it when we can.

✎ Action Step ✎

FOR YOUR ACTION Step, I'd like you to try praying either Morning or Evening Prayer before tomorrow. Most people aren't going to have a copy of the Liturgy of the Hours book lying around their house, but you can find the prayers at Divineoffice.org. There is also a wonderful "Sing the Hours" podcast that can help guide you in the Office, or you can find the hours prayed on Catholic prayer apps like Hallow.

If this is your first time attempting to pray the Liturgy of the Hours, don't worry too much at first about whether you are doing them right. Try your best to follow along with the website, app, podcast, or book that you are using, and if you keep working at it, you'll be doing it right in no time!

Going Deeper

THE RESOURCES I mentioned earlier are excellent places to start. You can also find a copy of the Liturgy of the Hours online or at a local Catholic bookstore. There is a one-volume book titled *Christian Prayer*, or you can get the more in-depth four-volume version. If you go this route, make sure the four-volume set is something you would use and enjoy, because it is an investment! There is also a monthly printing available from Word on Fire that you can get delivered every month, which also helps you learn more as you dive into this beautiful prayer of the Church.

Day 12

Lectio Divina

TODAY, WE'LL BE looking at an ancient method for reading Scripture called *lectio divina,* which translates from Latin to mean "divine reading." This beautiful way of praying with Scripture has existed in various forms since the early days of the Church. On Day 6, we explored the importance of the Bible and *why* we really should be taking time to read it. Today, we will look at how to read it in a way that helps it to penetrate our hearts more fully and teaches us how to *listen* to God's voice.

When we pray in this manner, we are not trying to read huge swaths of pages. Ideally, we should only pray with a single verse, paragraph, or at most a chapter at a time. There are four traditional steps to praying the *lecto divina* method, along with one additional step that is sometimes seen in more modern guides:

- *Lectio* (Reading) — First, we read the passage in order to understand what it is saying. What happened in the passage? What was its main message?
- *Meditatio* (Meditation) — Next, read the passage a second time and reflect on what we believe God might be trying to say directly to *us* through the passage. What deeper level of meaning is present? What truth does God want to reveal about Himself to you? What are some other ways you can

interpret the passage that weren't obvious on your first read-through?

- ✠ *Oratio* (Prayer) — Now take some time to enter into a prayer conversation with God about the passage and about what you felt or experienced during the *meditatio* step. Respond to God in your heart, ask questions, see if you hear His voice in some small way. If you'd like, you can read the passage again here, or allow certain sections or words to stand out to you.
- ✠ *Contemplatio* (Contemplation) — Read the passage once more, and allow yourself to be embraced by the Father's loving arms. Try to push aside distractions, anxieties, and anything that might be keeping you from allowing your mind and heart to be drawn deeper into the mystery of God. Recognize that God is present; rest and soak in the presence of the Holy Spirit.
- ✠ *Actio* (Action) — What are your takeaways from this time? Were there any changes that God was calling you to make? What concrete steps can you take to grow closer to God over the next few days?

These five steps can be summed up with the words Read, Reflect, Respond, Rest, and Resolve. It's that simple!

✎ Action Step ✎

FOR YOUR ACTION step today, you are going to try doing *lecto divina*. Open up your Bible to a passage of your choosing. I recommend starting with something from one of the four Gospels, especially if you aren't super experienced with navigating Scripture. Don't try to read a whole chapter, rather just a small section or paragraph. If you need a place to start, you can use one of the following passages:

- ✠ John 1:1–5 (The Word became flesh and dwelt among us)
- ✠ John 2:1–12 (The wedding at Cana, Jesus' first public miracle)
- ✠ Luke 15:11–32 (The parable of the prodigal son)
- ✠ Matthew 5:1–12 (The Beatitudes)
- ✠ Mark 6:30–44 (The feeding of the five thousand)

Scripture Passage ______________________________

- ✠ *Lectio* — What is the passage about? What happens?

____

____

____

____

____

- ✠ *Meditatio* — What is God trying to say to you? What is the main point or message?

____

____

____

____

- ✠ *Oratio* — What are some things you want to ask or say to God? How do you think He is answering you? Take time to enter into mental prayer and journal about what you experience during this time.

____

____

____

____

- ✠ *Contemplatio* — Take a moment to rest and be embraced by God.
- ✠ *Actio* — What are your biggest takeaways from this prayer time? What are some resolutions you want to make?

____

____

____

____

📖 Going Deeper 📖

IF YOU'D LIKE to go deeper, I simply recommend doing *lecto divina* more often. Many Bibles have a topical index if you are looking for a Scripture passage about a particular topic. You can also simply pick a book of the Bible such as a Gospel and work your way through it using this prayer method, or even flip the pages randomly until something strikes you and then enter into *lecto divina*. It's an ancient method of encountering God's Word, and I hope it helps you hear and listen to His voice.

PART 4

Benedictine Spirituality

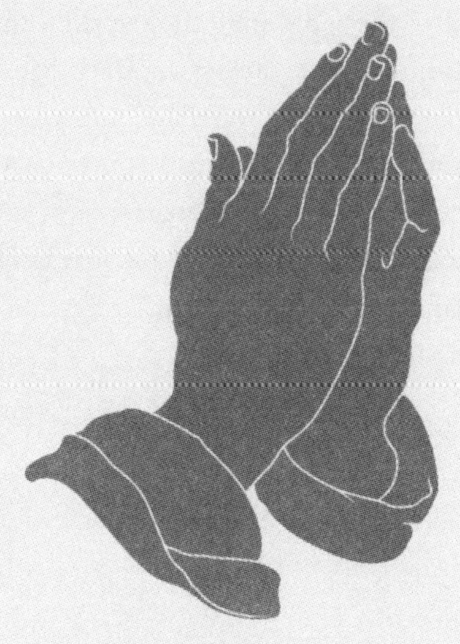

In this section we dive into Benedictine spirituality, the first of the major spiritualities that we cover. In the sixth century, Benedict of Nursia, like many holy men and women before him, left worldly living behind in order to begin a monastic life set apart for God. In time, several others joined him, and the Benedictine order was born. St. Benedict wrote a formal "rule" for monastic living, a document full of wisdom and advice for growing spiritually closer to God in community. In fact, it was actually within many of the Benedictine monasteries that the "Sacred and Traditional Methods of Prayer" from the last section really began to take shape before being embraced by the broader Church.

The Benedictine order grew rapidly as more and more monastic orders came into existence and adopted the *Rule of St. Benedict*. The influence that these monasteries had on world history cannot be overexaggerated — they became the world's first hospitals and schools and libraries. In fact, during the Dark Ages when civilization began to crumble, the monks were the ones who kept the seeds of rebirth alive in the books and culture that they protected within their walls. Many historians credit the monasteries as saving Western civilization — without them, most of the records before the Dark Ages would have been lost. For this reason, St. Benedict is actually given the title "patron saint of Europe."

Day 13

Gregorian Chant

MANKIND HAS ALWAYS used music as a way of trying to connect to the divine. In Judeo-Christian Tradition, we find this exemplified in ancient form most clearly through the psalms of the Old Testament. Though the melodies to these ancient Hebrew songs have been lost to history, their words have been memorialized in the book of Psalms in the Bible.

The Church also has a rich musical tradition that goes back centuries. The oldest form of this tradition (at least in the West) is known today as Gregorian chant, named after Pope St. Gregory the Great, who was Pope when this music was first cataloged.

Gregorian chant is most commonly found today in Benedictine monasteries. It is utilized most often during liturgical prayer, either at Mass or with the hymns and psalms of the Liturgy of the Hours. With true Gregorian chant, there is no musical accompaniment from an organ or any other musical instrument — it is produced only from the voices of those who are chanting. Some modern renditions use instruments.

A famous saying, often misattributed to St. Augustine, goes, "He who sings, prays twice." Though no hard evidence exists to attribute it to the saint (or anyone), there is certainly something to be said about this statement! Music has the power to open us up to experience God more deeply. Singing, of course, does not add anything to God's glory, but it does enable us to open our hearts up a little bit more to his grace.

There are two ways to pray with Gregorian chant — listening to it and learning it. Simply sitting and listening and allowing our hearts to be moved to a deeper appreciation of God's beauty and goodness is certainly a valid way to pray, and it can sanctify whatever we are doing. Playing chant in the background during household chores or while working can be a great way to keep our hearts engaged with the Lord, even while our minds are going through our task list for the day. For example, I wrote much of this book while listening to Gregorian chant playing in the background.

You can also try to learn some Gregorian chant. If you learn the words and translations as a form of prayer, you can engage the chant not only in your heart but in your mind as well. You can also learn to sing the chants. Although this takes patience and practice, it is a beautiful way to pray.

✎ Action Step ✎

YOUR ACTION STEP today requires some research. Your task is to find some Gregorian chant and try to pray with it. Try different versions until you find something that you enjoy. Feel free to use some of the resources in the Going Deeper section below.

Going Deeper

SOME OF MY favorite Gregorian chant albums are *CHANT: The Best of Gregorian Chant* by WordHarmonic and *Gregorian Chant* by the Monks of the Abbey of Notre Dame. *Gregorian Chant* by the Benedictine Monks of the Abbey of St. Maurice and St. Maur is also excellent.

If you're struggling to get into Gregorian chant, I encourage you to try listening to *Illumination: Peaceful Gregorian Chants* by Dan Gibson's Solitudes, which incorporates peaceful instrumentals as well as many sounds from nature alongside the chanting. Though purists may say it is not true Gregorian chant, it is a wonderful way to dip your toes into praying with chant. Finally, there is also a group called Catholic Lofi that offers a unique genre of Gregorian chant mixed with some soothing instrumental pieces and lofi hiphop beats. It's definitely worth checking out. The album *This Sacred Heart* by them is a great place to start.

If you'd like to learn more about actually participating in Gregorian chant and learning how to chant these ancient prayers, I recommend the *Chant School Podcast* by Floriani. In addition to their podcast and albums, they also have courses available online that go a little bit more in-depth if this is something that you want to pursue. You can find this all at https://www.floriani.org/.

Day 14

Ora et Labora

ONE OF THE key principles of Benedictine spirituality is found in their motto, "Ora et Labora," a Latin phrase that means "Pray and work." For St. Benedict, prayer and work were two sides of the same coin, and both were required of his monks. Monastic life in the Benedictine abbeys consisted of praying the Liturgy of the Hours (which is the work of God), academic study, and some sort of manual labor. Benedict's *Rule* called for a balance between these two. In Chapter 48 of the *Rule*, he warns that "idleness is the enemy of the soul" and gives strict instruction that the monks are called to "live by the labor of their hands, as our fathers and the apostles did."[21] Benedictine monks often farm and grow everything they need for their bodily nourishment, but they often also specialize in a craft or trade that they offer to the broader community to financially support their monastery. You may have heard that monks make the best beer, cheese, and coffee, but you can also find Benedictine communities that make olive oil, mustard, chocolate, clothes, and honey!

For those who follow a Benedictine spirituality, the process of creating these goods is not simply a fun pastime; it is a labor of love and an offering to God. God is invited into the process, and the work itself *becomes* the prayer. Note, however, that this work doesn't

[21] *The Rule of St. Benedict in English*, ed. Timothy Fry, O. S. B. (Collegeville, MN: Liturgical Press, 1982).

replace the structured times of prayer (the Liturgy of the Hours), but rather having these structured times of prayer throughout the day helps to elevate the times of work. There are also other methods of prayer that we can bring into our times of work to help sanctify it. Listening to Gregorian chant or other sacred music is one such way. Another could be praying the Rosary (which we talk more about on Day 37), or utilizing another vocal prayer. Others might simply engage in mental prayer, speaking to God from their heart and allowing themselves to rest peacefully in His presence while their hands work.

There are many ways that we can utilize this Benedictine spiritual practice in our daily life. We all have chores that need to be done, and many of us have hobbies that involve artistic talent or craftsmanship. The "work of our hands" can also be our day job! The means by which we provide for ourselves and our families can become sanctified and turned into a prayer. Some simple ways we can do this is by taking little breaks throughout the day to say prayers of gratitude to God, continually inviting his presence into our work, and listening to spiritual music while we work.

✎ Action Step ✎

YOUR ACTION STEP today is to do some chores, but instead of doing them in a mindless fashion or with a TV show or secular music in the background, I'd like you to practice allowing the work itself to become a prayer and offering to God. Choose a household task that you've been putting off, or set aside fifteen minutes to clean, organize, or do some yard work. If you are artistic or crafty, feel free to use your artistic talents to work on something during this time. Say a prayer beforehand asking the Lord to sanctify this time, and then reflect on the goodness and love of God while you work. If it's beneficial for you to do so, play some Gregorian chant or simply allow your mind to rest while your hands work. Be at peace knowing you are surrounded by the presence of God who sustains you and gives you life.

Going Deeper

IF YOU'D LIKE to learn more about Benedictine spirituality, I recommend *The Benedictine Handbook* (edited by Anthony Marett-Crosby), which is filled with reflections and prayer materials to take a deeper dive into this tradition. You can also go back to the primary source and read the *Rule of St. Benedict* itself, but keep in mind that it was written primarily for monks and some of the practices contained within it won't be applicable to the life of the average layperson. Chapter 48 of the *Rule* in particular speaks to the importance of *ora et labora* in the Benedictine lifestyle.

PART 5

Carmelite Spirituality

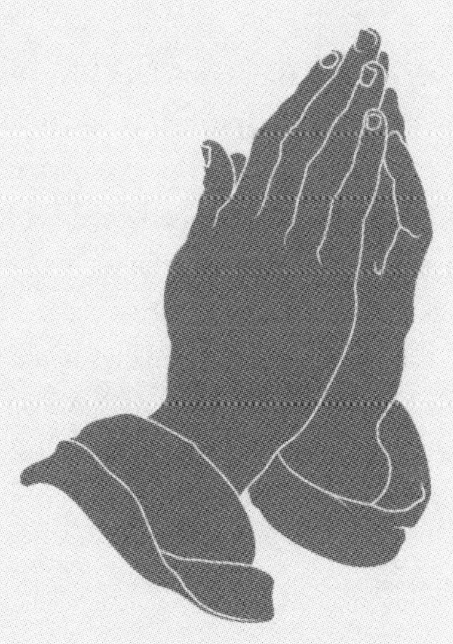

THE CARMELITE ORDER traces its roots back to the ancient monastic tradition. It receives its name not from an individual, like many of the other orders in this book, but rather from a place: Mount Carmel. Located in modern-day Palestine, Mount Carmel is most closely connected with the prophet Elijah, who we read briefly about on Day 10. It is the place where Elijah confronted and defeated the false prophets of Baal.

In the late twelfth century, a group of hermits settled on Mount Carmel and built a chapel dedicated to the Blessed Mother. Over time, a small monastic community began to form and seek a formal rule for living. They became an official religious order in 1247, when Pope Innocent IV gave his approval. Though the Carmelites don't have a true "founder" in the sense that the other religious orders in this book do, they consider themselves followers of Elijah and try to emulate his zeal.

One of the key reasons the Carmelites have remained so popular is because of the magnificent spiritual writings of Carmelite saints, especially St. John of the Cross, St. Teresa of Ávila, and St. Thérèse of Lisieux. Each of these saints is so renowned for his or her spiritual works that each has been given the title of "Doctor of the Church," and their writings are considered spiritual classics.

One of the things that sets Carmelites apart from some of the other orders is that they place a great emphasis on mystical theology and focus on the soul becoming perfectly united to God. We'll be unpacking what this means over the course of the next couple of days.

Day 15

Finding God in Solitude

TODAY WE'RE GOING to take an in-depth look at the power of *solitude*. In general, the Carmelite orders tend to be slightly more cloistered than other orders. In many cases (especially with religious sisters), Carmelites may spend their whole life in their cloister. While other religious orders often have an emphasis on some sort of active work for the betterment of society, such as education or serving the poor directly, the true "work" of the Carmelite is to pray. In a special way, Carmelites are set apart from the world in order to more perfectly unite themselves to God.

With that being said, many branches of Carmelites do various works of mercy in the world, and there are also third-order Carmelites composed of laypeople striving to actively integrate Carmelite spirituality into daily life. Though most of us won't live a cloistered life, we can take away certain principles from their rule, one of which is the importance of taking time for solitude with God.

On Day 10, we looked at Elijah as an example of the importance of silence in the spiritual life. It's worth noting also that he went on the journey alone. When we speak of being alone, we should distinguish between two very different forms that this can take: isolation and solitude. Though on the surface the two look very similar, each actually points to a very different internal experience, both psychologically and spiritually.

To be in isolation means to be cut off. When we are in a state of isolation, we experience the pain of loneliness. We recognize this as something bad, contrary to who we are as human beings. We learn, in a painful way, the timeless truth that "it is not good that the man should be alone" (Gen. 2:18, RSVCE).

Solitude, on the other hand, denotes something deeper than merely a psychological experience of loneliness. Rather than the feeling of being cut off, solitude can be described as the experience of being set apart. In his Theology of the Body Wednesday audiences, Pope St. John Paul II referred to an "original solitude," the experience that Adam had in recognizing that he was like nothing else in creation. It is only in recognizing his own uniqueness that he came to know himself consciously as a *person*, something more than animal, a being made in the image and likeness of God.[22]

In other words, *only when we stand alone in solitude before God are we able to see ourselves as we truly are.*

As we explored on Day 8, community is a fundamental part of Christian life. We need others on our spiritual journey. It takes a village to raise young disciples. Indeed, it is truly *not* good for man to be alone. But in solitude, we learn how to experience true peace and freedom. By spending intentional time alone, away from technology and distractions, we give ourselves the opportunity to grow in self-knowledge and encounter God. We are trained to be still and experience deeper peace. We learn how to live with ourselves, and love ourselves in a healthy way, which helps us to love others as well.

There will come a time when each of us finds ourselves very much alone. When everything and everyone is stripped away from us for a time and we stand naked before our Creator, we discover who we are. This experience will be felt most prominently at the moment

[22] John Paul II, General Audience (October 10, 1979).

of our death, when we stand before the throne of God and await judgment at the ultimate moment of solitude, when we are either admitted into the community of heaven or the isolation of hell.

Time spent in solitude prepares us for this moment and helps us to see it as a gift. This is why each of us should set ourselves apart to be alone with God. One of the best things we can do for our spiritual life is to take a spiritual retreat from time to time. The vast majority of us live our lives in a world of busyness and noise. A retreat is an opportunity to take a step back from that world into solitude to be alone with God. In military terms, a retreat is often a strategic maneuver; something done in order to recoup to get back in the fight. A spiritual retreat likewise allows us to step away from the world to allow ourselves to be filled up with God's presence.

Carmelites are set apart to pray always and intercede for the world. Those of us who live in the world also need to take some time to recharge if we want to avoid burnout, both in a mental sense and a spiritual one. Indeed, taking time to be in solitude with God is crucial to our spiritual health.

Action Step

TAKE SOME TIME to schedule a spiritual retreat during the next year. Look up some Catholic retreat centers in your area, or plan a time to get away at a camp, monastery, church, or other place where you can be alone for a day or weekend. Your goal is to get away from technology and other people and focus in solitude on your relationship with God.

Alternatively, if you absolutely cannot get away, plan your own spiritual retreat. Find a local parish that has Adoration hours, and commit to at least one or two hours of silent and personal prayer before the Blessed Sacrament sometime soon.

Either way, write down your plan below and get it on your calendar!

____

____

____

____

Going Deeper

A BOOK TITLED *Solitude and Silence: The Cloister of the Heart* by Thomas à Kempis dives a bit deeper into today's ideas. Several books found on the list in the back and in other sections of this book also speak on the importance of solitude, especially many of the Carmelites' books, such as *Interior Castle* by St. Teresa of Ávila.

Day 16

Embracing the Little Way

OF ALL OF the Carmelite saints, perhaps the most widely known and loved is St. Thérèse of Lisieux. In fact, she is one of the most beloved saints in modern times, and countless books and resources are available about her unique contributions to Catholic spirituality. Known as the "Little Flower," she lived a cloistered life away from the world and died at the age of twenty-four. While she was alive, her superiors requested that she keep a journal and write an autobiography. This book, titled *The Story of a Soul,* is an in-depth look at the spiritual life of one of the greatest modern saints. From the time she entered the convent at the age of fifteen, St. Thérèse never set foot outside of her Carmelite cloister, yet her message has spread across the world. Today she is even known as the patron saint of missionaries.

The crux of St. Thérèse's "little way" is that we should aim to become one of God's "little *ones*." Instead of striving to do great acts that will leave our fingerprint on history, we should strive to do "small things with great love," to quote a motto attributed to Mother Teresa (who chose her name because of the inspiration of St. Thérèse!). St. Thérèse believed that trying to climb the steps of perfection and holiness was nearly impossible. In her own words, she sought an elevator by which she might be perfected more quickly.[23]

[23] Thérèse of Lisieux, *Story of a Soul,* 117.

Searching the Bible she came upon Proverbs 9:4: "Whoever is a little one, let him come to me."[24] It was here that she found her elevator! Instead of working hard at climbing the steps of holiness, we should strive to become one of God's little ones. This is the genius of St. Thérèse. We do not have to fight and spend countless energies trying to perfect ourselves; we merely need to surrender and allow Jesus to lift us up to the heights of perfection by *His* power. We must become small to be made great. Like the wedding guest who takes the lowest seat of honor in the parable in Luke 14, we should strive to humble ourselves in order to be lifted to the heights of our greatest potential.

What does this look like practically? First and foremost, it means that we have to accept ourselves and all of our weaknesses. We recognize that we aren't perfect, and we need to be patient with ourselves. Jesus commanded us to "be perfect," but He didn't say, "Be perfect *now.*" He knows us better than we know ourselves. "For he knows our frame; he remembers that we are but dust" (Ps. 103:14, RSVCE). He loves us as we are, and accepting His love is the key to becoming *more* than we are, which leads us to the second point: we must learn to trustfully abandon ourselves with all of these weaknesses and imperfections into the hands of God. Holiness is something God does in us, not something we achieve on our own. Surrendering ourselves in trust to the Lord: this is what the Little Way is all about.

[24] This is the translation from Thérèse of Lisieux, *Story of a Soul*, 117. The RSVCE translation reads, "Whoever is simple, let him turn in here!"

✎ Action Step ✎

TAKE SOME TIME to write your own prayer of surrender in the style of St. Thérèse. You can word it any way you'd like, but try to hit the main points:

- ✠ I know I'm not perfect, but I know You love me anyway.
- ✠ I surrender and I give You permission to work in my heart as You see fit.

Use your prayer journal or the space below to write out your prayer.

____

____

____

____

____

____

____

📖 Going Deeper 📖

SEVERAL FINE BOOKS can help you live out this spirituality if it's something you feel called to pursue:

- *The Story of a Soul* by St. Thérèse of Lisieux is a wonderful autobiography and spiritual classic.
- *33 Days to Merciful Love* by Fr. Michael Gaitley takes the spirituality of St. Thérèse and breaks it down over the course of thirty-three days of reflection in a do-it-yourself style of retreat.
- *Abandonment to Divine Providence* by Jean-Pierre de Caussade is another classic that has a lot of similarities to the Little Way spirituality. It is a book that will certainly challenge you spiritually, but it is well worth reading if you feel called to live out the Carmelite charism of surrendering more fully to God's will for your life.

Day 17

Intercessory Prayer

IF YOU GREW up Catholic, there's a strong chance that before going to bed each night you recited the classic "God bless Mommy, Daddy, Baby, Grandpa, Grandma, Uncle George, etc." prayer. This is intercessory prayer in its most simple form.

Essentially, intercessory prayer means praying on behalf of another. This often takes the form of praying for someone to receive healing, conversion, or some other material or spiritual blessing. Praying deeply for others has long been a tradition of Carmelite spirituality, and the Carmelites especially pray for healing and conversion in the world. Intercessory prayer is a key part of the Carmelite goal of becoming more perfectly united to God, because, as the Catechism of the Catholic Church reminds us, "since Abraham, intercession — asking on behalf of another — has been characteristic of a heart attuned to God's mercy." Furthermore, when we pray for others, we are following the example that Christ set forth in Scripture (CCC 2635).

Intercessory prayer is effective, and it is powerful. Many powerful figures throughout history, including some saints, can attribute their conversion to the prayers of an intercessory figure. The most famous example of this is probably St. Monica's prayers for her son Augustine. Augustine is renowned as one of the greatest Catholic saints and theologians who has ever lived. However, as a young man his lifestyle was anything but saintly. Augustine lived a life focused primarily on moving from pleasure to pleasure, with no regard for Christianity. But his mother, Monica, was devout, and prayed unceasingly for her son day after day. Eventually, her prayers were answered; Augustine not only converted to the Faith in a seemingly miraculous way, he also became one of the most significant Fathers and Doctors of the Church!

Intercessory prayer can be addressed directly to God, or we can also ask other people to join us in our prayers, including the angels and saints. Countless stories of healings are attributed to the prayers of saints, both during and after their lives, since these saints continue to pray for us from heaven! Yet a lot of people ask, especially if they grew up in a background outside of the Catholic or Orthodox Church, "Why ask for prayers from the saints or from others? Why not go directly to God?"

All Christians, living and dead, are united to Jesus in a mysterious and sacramental manner by virtue of our Baptism. We are active members of Christ's Body, and we pray with His Spirit. When we pray in an intercessory manner for others, we join ourselves to His intercessory prayer for all mankind, and His Holy Spirit actively prays in and through us. Priests, in a special manner, enter even more deeply into Christ's intercessory prayer, especially through the Holy Sacrifice of the Mass, as they offer themselves along with Christ in a sacrificial-intercessory manner, uniting themselves to Jesus on the Cross. We also believe that the saints, who are with God in Heaven, have a special intercessory power by virtue of their holy witness and the fact that they now spend all their time in prayer before God. When we ask the saints to pray for us, they cannot get distracted or forget: they are eternally in the presence of God, worshiping, praising, and praying! As the *Catechism* teaches,

> The witnesses who have preceded us into the kingdom, especially those whom the Church recognizes as saints, share in the living tradition of prayer by the example of their lives, the transmission of their writings, and their prayer today. They contemplate God, praise him and constantly care for those whom they have left on earth.... Their intercession is their most exalted service to God's plan. We can and should ask them to intercede for us and for the whole world. (CCC 2683)

Intercessory prayer is powerful. When we pray for others, it truly makes a difference. Even a simple prayer asking for mercy for someone who hurt us or a prayer for someone to experience the grace of coming to know God can bear tremendous fruit. When we unite ourselves to God, incredible and miraculous things can happen. Of course, the highest form of intercessory prayer is the Mass, which is why it is so important for us to have Masses said for our loved ones, and it is so important for our parish priests to dedicate Masses to their parish communities.

Yesterday, we took a brief look at St. Thérèse's Little Way of uniting herself to God. Today we conclude by briefly recounting a story from her younger years:

> As I closed my Missal after Mass one Sunday, a picture of the Crucifixion slipped out a little way, and I could just see one of the wounds in Our Lord's hands, with blood flowing from it. A strange new thrill passed over me. It pierced my heart with sorrow to see His Precious Blood falling, with no one bothering to catch it, and I made up my mind, there and then, to stay in spirit at the foot of the Cross, to gather up the dew of heavenly life and give it to others.
>
> The cry of Jesus as He died, "I thirst," echoed every moment in my soul, inflaming my heart with a burning love. I

> longed to satisfy His thirst for souls; I was consumed myself with the same thirst, and yearned to save them from the everlasting flames of Hell, no matter what the cost.[25]

Thérèse then goes on to recount a story about a hardened criminal named Pranzini, condemned to death for murder and showing no signs of repentance. Thérèse prayed for God to forgive him, asking in complete trust that it would happen but also asking the Lord to give a sign of his repentance. The next day, she read the paper and saw that at the moment before his execution Pranzini turned to the priest holding a crucifix close by and kissed the wounds of Christ three times. For Thérèse, this was the answer to her prayer for a sign, since it was the sight of the Sacred Wounds that inspired in her a thirst for souls.

Note how this intercessory experience encouraged a deep longing in Little Thérèse's heart to pray for others. It certainly played a part in her discovering her vocation. Though we are all certainly called to pray for each other and for others, as we grow in prayer, we will learn that certain individuals have a specific call to a formal and integrated approach to this type of prayer.

[25] Thérèse of Lisieux, *Story of a Soul*, 54–55.

Action Step

MAKE AN INTERCESSORY prayer plan. Who do you feel called to pray for in a special way? How are you going to go about praying for this person? Some common ways include praying a Rosary or Divine Mercy Chaplet, having a Mass said, making some sort of spiritual sacrifice or fast, or simply asking God in your own words to be with this person and his or her needs. Use the space below to make a plan or to write out your prayer for this person.

___

___

___

___

___

___

___

Going Deeper

THE BOOK *INTERCESSION: A Guide to Effective Prayer* by Sr. Ann Shields is filled with practical steps for how to more effectively pray for others and build intercessory prayer habits into your life. It also explains the theology of why intercessory prayer is so important. I highly recommend it for anyone who feels called to learn how to pray more effectively for others.

Day 18

Practicing the Presence of God

ON OUR FINAL day focusing on Carmelite spirituality, we're going to explore practicing the presence of God. This phrase comes from a book called *The Practice of the Presence of God* written by Brother Lawrence, a Carmelite friar who lived during the seventeenth century and who was known for his austere holiness and spiritual advice. The book itself is a simple collection of conversations and letters from Brother Lawrence. The practice of the presence of God is also simple, at least in theory. It simply means to be aware at all times and in every moment that God is with us. The man who compiled these conversations and letters of Brother Lawrence wrote,

> His view of prayer was nothing else but a sense of the presence of GOD, his soul being at that time insensible to everything but Divine love. That when the appointed times of prayer were passed, he found no difference, because he still continued with GOD, praising and blessing Him with all his might, so that he passed his life in continual joy.[26]

Brother Lawrence sought one thing and one thing only: to be wholly God's. This is, of course, much easier said than done. Yet it is exactly

[26] Brother Lawrence, *The Practice of the Presence of God*, new and rev. ed. with an additional letter ([1906] Ireland: CrossReach Publications, 2022), 19.

what St. Paul wrote of when he said to "pray without ceasing" (1 Thess. 5:17, NABRE). Brother Lawrence's state of life and his vocation as a religious brother facilitated the encounter and experience for him to pursue his goal successfully, but most of us don't share his same background or vocation. Even so, there is still much to be gained from trying to attain the practice of the presence of God.

First off, as I already alluded to, we should eagerly strive for this awareness of God's presence at all times. We should actively seek to cultivate an interior thirst for the Lord. We also need to recognize that without allotting certain periods of time to prayer, attaining this level of depth and interiority with God is impossible. In fact, one could even argue that the whole point of this book is to help you discover the methods of prayer that allow you to have this continued experience of God's presence throughout the day.

It should also be noted that, true to its name, this really does *take practice*. None of us can achieve such holiness in a day, and it is likely none of us will be able to do so perfectly. Yet the effort in itself is commendable, and simply trying to maintain this prayerful awareness of God throughout the day is certain to bear lots of fruit in our lives. Think of how much we can grow in holiness and in conquering our vices simply by maintaining a prayerful awareness and connection to God's presence! Practicing the presence of God truly has the power to radically transform our spirituality and the lens through which we view life.

Action Step

MAKE A RESOLUTION to try practicing the presence of God for the rest of the day (or all of tomorrow if you are reading this shortly before bed). Make sure to take some solid, allotted prayer time, and then do your best to prayerfully recognize God's presence at all times throughout the day. Use the space below to journal about the experience: your successes and victories as well as the areas where you fell short. If you felt like you conversed with God throughout the day, write a little bit about that experience here as well.

____

____

____

____

____

____

____

Going Deeper

TO LEARN MORE about this devotion, I encourage you to read from the primary source itself. *The Practice of the Presence of God* by Brother Lawrence is a timeless spiritual classic that includes several accounts about the good brother's spiritual practice along with some letters that he wrote about it. It is easily accessible online in the public domain.

PART 6

Franciscan Spirituality

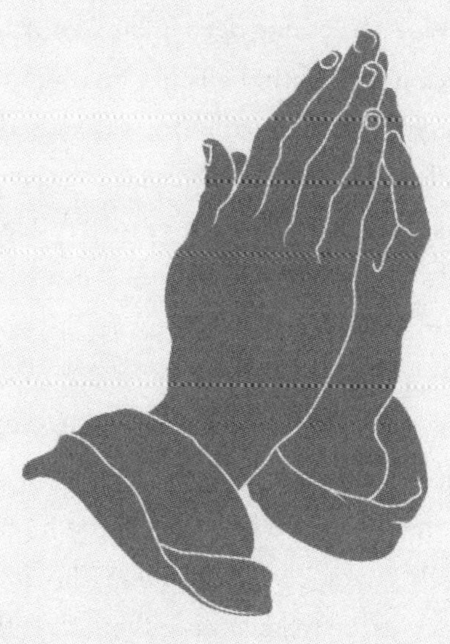

When people hear of St. Francis, the first thing they often think of is his popular depiction with songbirds and baby animals. Though he is the patron saint of animals and animal lovers, St. Francis is so much more than simply a man who loved animals; he was a man who passionately loved God and quite literally gave up everything in order to try and follow Him more perfectly. He was able to see the face of Christ in the lowliest among us, the lepers and the outcasts of society. He was able to see God's beauty and grace in the lowliest of creatures and in every created thing, no matter how small or seemingly insignificant.

Francis began his life as the son of a noble merchant. He lived a life of luxury and licentiousness and embraced the worldliness and worldly success that his father pressed upon him. He discovered in himself a hunger for something deeper, but instead of turning toward a deeper embrace of the Catholic Faith, he sought glory on the battlefield as a knight. Unfortunately for Francis, the small army of Assisi was brutally defeated and he was taken prisoner by a neighboring city until his ransom was paid a year later. He went back to his partying lifestyle and sought glory once more on the battlefield when the call for the Fourth Crusade came. But when he was a day's journey away from the city, Francis had a dream in which God told him to turn back. This was the beginning of Francis's conversion.

One day in a small, dilapidated chapel, St. Francis heard the voice of God come from the crucifix, telling him, "Francis, rebuild my church, which as you can see is falling down." Taking the voice literally, St. Francis set to work at once rebuilding the small chapel. It was only much later that he realized he was being called to rebuild the *whole* Church.

Francis eventually gave up everything to follow Jesus. Inspired by Francis's example and his preaching, others began to follow him and a brotherhood was formed. This brotherhood extended not only to every human person he encountered but to every created thing.

St. Francis saw his life as part of the interconnected tapestry of God's creation. There are legends that revolve around him preaching to birds and domesticating a wolf, which is why he's often pictured with animals. He was also the first known saint to experience the sacred stigmata; the wounds of Christ miraculously and mystically appeared on his body while he prayed to share more deeply in Christ's suffering. He was a man who conformed himself completely to Christ, and he is considered one of the greatest saints in the Church.

St. Francis wanted the radical freedom of loving God and God alone. The movement that he started transformed the face of the Church (and the world) and helped lead to incredible renewal and reformation. In a modern world that is immersed so heavily in materialism and consumerism, we need his prayers more than ever. St. Francis, pray for us!

Day 19

Embracing Lady Poverty

FOR ST. FRANCIS, one of the surest ways to follow Jesus was to totally embrace poverty. In fact, he often referred to poverty as "lady poverty" and spoke of her with great affection. Growing up, Francis lived a life of the highest luxury, but as he grew deeper in his faith, he often gave things away, which greatly angered his father, who brought him publicly before the bishop and demanded that Francis stop behaving this way. At that moment, Francis gave everything he owned to his father, even the clothes he was wearing, and surrendered his right to inheritance. Wearing nothing but rags, he exclaimed, "Pietro Bernardone is no longer my father. From now on I can say with complete freedom, 'Our Father who art in heaven.'" He never truly owned anything ever again. He became a beggar and lived only off of the food that was given to him or that was donated to the brotherhood.

For St. Francis, poverty was a way of imitating Christ. Biblical scholars have long pointed out that there is evidence in Scripture that Jesus grew up in an extremely modest home. The offering of turtledoves by St. Joseph, for example, instead of lambs would have been characteristic of families who could not afford the preferred sacrificial animals. During his public ministry, Jesus Himself remarked, "Foxes have holes, and birds of the air have nests; but the Son of man has nowhere to lay his head" (Matt. 8:20, RSVCE).

For Francis and his followers, the absence of material possessions meant a *lack of attachment* to material possessions. They believed that by giving up material things, they were able to experience the true spiritual freedom promised by Jesus: "Blessed are the poor in spirit, for theirs is the kingdom of heaven" (Matt. 5:3, RSVCE).

How many of us today feel "possessed" by our possessions? In the modern world, many people are trying to combat this mindset by gravitating toward a more minimalist lifestyle of few possessions. Such people may find great comfort in Franciscan spirituality, which places an emphasis on the freedom of life without attachment to material things. But for Franciscans, this lack of possessions is not simply about mental health — it is about experiencing the power of freedom from materialism and aiding our ability to experience God in His fullness.

Action Step

TAKE SOME TIME to reflect on your attachment to various possessions that you own. Though not everyone is called to the radical poverty of St. Francis (especially with the demands of family life and providing for children), we *all* should seek a healthy level of detachment. Where is there room for growth in this area of your life? Use the space below to write out some of your thoughts, and take some time to pray for a spirit of detachment.

____

____

____

____

Going Deeper

THE BOOK *Happy Are You Poor: The Simple Life and Spiritual Freedom* by Thomas Dubay is an excellent analysis of the beatitude "Blessed are the poor" and shows us how to live it out more fully. There is also a growing movement toward minimalism in the modern world, which emphasizes not being overly attached to material possessions. With a little intentionality, implementing principles of minimalism can become a form of Franciscan prayer and spirituality.

Day 20

Encountering God in Nature

WITHOUT MATERIAL POSSESSIONS weighing them down, St. Francis and his brothers were free to experience God in a spirit of total freedom. Instead of spending time focused on human creations, they entered most fully into God's Creation. All of the beauty of the natural world was theirs to experience. In one sense, it was really all they had.

If you ever get the chance to visit Assisi where St. Francis and his companions lived, you'll find at once that it is a place of supreme natural beauty. For Francis, the beauty of Creation was a reflection of the innate beauty of the Creator. For centuries, Christians had retreated into the wilderness to experience God in the wonders of the natural world, but in Francis, this experience reached new heights through his appreciation of the beauty that he found there.

Mankind has nearly always sought to control nature and bend it to our own will, and the modern world often sees the natural world as something that is extrinsic, outside of us. Science has become a tool to work against our nature and try to control it. We see countless examples of this attempt at control in things like toxic pesticides that do more harm than good, hormonal medicines and treatments that damage or suppress our natural rhythms (or even cause various types of cancer), and many other procedures, treatments, and unnatural techniques that have become a routine part of modern, daily operations.

The Franciscan view, on the other hand, is to see ourselves as part of nature, not something separate from it. Everything is interconnected, everything has one thing in common — being *created*. In this lens, we should strive to live as "naturally" as possible. The Bible is clear that we have been given dominion over nature and the natural world (see Gen. 1:26), but this doesn't mean we subdue the world to do whatever we wish. Instead, we are the *caretakers* of nature and the natural world, and we should strive to live in perfect harmony with it.

The Franciscan way of viewing the world finds its culmination in St. Francis's famous poem *The Canticle of the Sun*. This song of praise of God for His creation is actually the very first recorded poem in the Italian language. Here is the full text of this beautiful prayer:

Most High, all-powerful, good Lord,
Yours are the praises, the glory, the honor, and all blessings.

To You alone, Most High, do they belong,
and no man is worthy to mention Your name.

Praised be You, my Lord, with all your creatures;
especially Brother Sun, who is the day,
and through whom You give us light.

And he is beautiful and radiant with great splendor,
and bears a likeness to You, Most High One.

Praised be You, my Lord, through Sister Moon and the stars;
in heaven You formed them clear and precious and beautiful.

Praised be You, my Lord, through Brother Wind,
and through the air, cloudy and serene,
and every kind of weather through which
You give sustenance to Your creatures.

Praised be You, my Lord, through Sister Water,
which is very useful and humble and precious and chaste.

Praised be You, my Lord, through Brother Fire,
through whom You light the night;
and he is beautiful and playful and robust and strong.

Praised be You, my Lord, through Sister Mother Earth,
who sustains us and governs us and who produces
varied fruits with colored flowers and herbs.

Praised be You, my Lord,
through those who give pardon for Your love,
and bear infirmity and tribulation.

Blessed are those who endure in peace
for by You, Most High, they shall be crowned.

Praised be You, my Lord,
through our Sister Bodily Death,
from whom no living man can escape.

Woe to those who die in mortal sin.
Blessed are those whom death will find in Your most holy will,
for the second death shall do them no harm.

Praise and bless my Lord,
and give Him thanks,
and serve Him with great humility.

Amen.[27]

[27] St. Francis, *The Canticle of the Sun*, The Franciscan Friars, accessed November 27, 2024, https://franciscanfriarscresson.org/the-canticle-of-the-sun/.

Action Step

Today you get to choose between two options. The first is to go back and read *The Canticle of the Sun* again and reflect on the unique worldview that St. Francis is revealing in it. The second is to put your phone on silent for a time and go on a nature walk, admiring the beauty of creation and thanking the Creator for making it. Feel free to use the space below to write about your experience.

____

____

____

____

Going Deeper

If you'd like to learn more about encountering God in nature, I encourage you to begin by spending time with God in nature. Try taking some of the other prayer methods from this book and combining them with a hike or walk in the woods. I also would highly recommend the papal encyclical *Laudato Si'* written by Pope Francis if you'd like to do a deeper dive into mankind's relationship with (and responsibility toward) creation and nature.

Day 21

Praising God through Song

WE ENDED YESTERDAY'S reflection with the lyrics of a medieval song written by St. Francis. Today, we look more into the tradition of sacred music. It's clear from many accounts of Francis's life that he and his brother Franciscans were accustomed to singing songs of praise to God while out in the wilderness. Oftentimes, these songs appeared to be almost spontaneous — the cry of a heart for the thing it loves most.

The simple expression of prayer in song reveals a deep truth about who we are as human beings. We have archaeological evidence of music as a crucial part of human society from every major culture and time period. Since the beginning of civilization, music has also been involved in worship in some capacity. The reason for this is simple — music is *powerful*. It draws our hearts into prayer and moves us emotionally and spiritually. It takes us outside of ourselves and helps us enter into a mindset of praise.

I remember many years ago when my wife and I were preparing for marriage, one of our marriage course instructors taught us that "loving feelings follow loving actions." In other words, we shouldn't wait until we *feel* love before showing love to our spouse with words of affirmation, giving gifts, and spending time with him or her. It is often after we make an act of the will to show our spouse love that the feeling of love fills our hearts. This principle applies to our relationship with God as well. We are commanded to love God with our heart, mind, soul, and strength (see Deut. 6:5; Mark 12:30), and one of the key ways we can train our hearts to love Him is by making an act of the will to praise Him. Praise is using words of affirmation to tell God how wonderful He is. Our ability to praise God is a beautiful gift, since we praise God for our sake; our praise does not and cannot add glory to God.

Praise opens outward the door of our hearts. When those doors open, God is able to enter more deeply and rest in our souls. When we combine music and praise, we find a powerful recipe for experiencing God's love! Singing, playing, and listening to songs of praise are wonderful methods of prayer. St. Francis was no stranger to this idea. It is said that he could often be heard singing songs of praise while traveling, and we saw in yesterday's reflection that he even wrote a beloved song of praise himself.

As a musician myself, I can attest to the power of incorporating music into prayer. In a particular way, I have seen praise and worship music transform hearts and minds and draw people young and old into a deeper desire for God. God is the source of everything that is good, true, and beautiful. Music is like a lens through which we can experience God's beauty. When beautiful music is coupled with lyrics proclaiming truth about who God is and how good He is, we provide an opportunity for hearts and minds to be transformed.

✎ Action Step ✎

YOUR ACTION STEP today is to take some time to listen to some sacred music. Because there are countless genres (ranging from ancient chant to folk to synth-pop contemporary Christian music and everything in between!), here are a few places to start.

If you enjoy classical or more traditional music or are just learning about it, I recommend the following pieces:

- ✠ *Requiem in D Minor, K. 626,* by Wolfgang Amadeus Mozart
- ✠ *Messiah, HVW 56* by George Frideric Handel
- ✠ *St. Matthew Passion, BVW 244* by Johann Sebastian Bach
- ✠ *A German Requiem, To Words of the Holy Scriptures, Op. 45* by Johannes Brahms
- ✠ *Locus Este, WAB 23* by Anton Bruckner

If you like more contemporary music, I recommend Damascus Worship, a Catholic missionary worship movement. Matt Maher is another excellent contemporary Catholic musician worth checking out.

Going Deeper

THERE ARE SO many wonderful pieces of music out there that can lift our hearts in prayer. Though many Christian radio stations tend to play the same style or genre of praise and worship music, there is a lot of independent Christian music out there, with songs of praise really being found in just about every genre of music imaginable. Of course, there is also a vast treasury to be found in the Church's rich tradition of sacred music. I would encourage you to find some uplifting music that fits your particular musical taste and incorporate it into your day.

Day 22

Becoming an Instrument of Peace

St. Francis had quite the reputation for helping people achieve peace with one another (and even with animals, in some cases!). He was able to facilitate peace for others because of the deep peace that he carried within his own heart. Francis had given away everything he owned to embrace God alone. This poverty of spirit allowed him to be unshaken by the world and maintain internal peace, even in the face of hardship. This experience of internal peace allowed Francis to bring God's peace everywhere he went.

There are countless stories that tell of Francis's peacemaking roles. For example, during the Fifth Crusade, St. Francis journeyed to the Egyptian city of Damietta, which was under siege. Francis and his companion left the Christian camp and walked right into the heart of the Muslim camp to speak to the sultan. Instead of having Francis executed, the sultan recognized Francis's holiness and treated him as an esteemed guest. Many conversations took place between the two over the week that Francis spent there. In addition to preaching the gospel and explaining the Christian Faith, Francis also spent time begging for peace between the two warring factions.

Another popular story tells of Francis bringing peace between a small village and a wolf that was eating the town's livestock. Francis tamed and domesticated the wolf, which in turn was taken care of by the town, almost as a sort of mascot.

When Jesus sent His disciples out among the towns, He told them to "let their peace" rest upon the households where they went, and in His Sermon on the Mount, he told his followers, "Blessed are the peacemakers" (Matt. 5:9, RSVCE). St. Francis certainly was blessed, and he blessed many people during his lifetime through his role as peacemaker. We too are blessed when we seek to become instruments of God's peace. Indeed, when we carry peace within us, we carry the presence of the Holy Spirit, who empowers us to share God's love and peace with others.

We truly see St. Francis's desire to bring peace to others most in a famous prayer that he wrote. This prayer is a fitting conclusion to today's reflection:

Lord, make me an instrument of your peace.
Where there is hatred, let me sow love;
where there is injury, pardon;
where there is doubt, faith;
where there is despair, hope;
where there is darkness, light;
and where there is sadness, joy.

O Divine Master, grant that I may not so much seek
to be consoled as to console;
to be understood as to understand;
to be loved as to love.
For it is in giving that we receive;
it is in pardoning that we are pardoned;
and it is in dying that we are born to eternal life.

Amen.[28]

[28] "Pray with St. Francis," The Franciscan Friars, accessed November 27, 2024, https://franciscanfriarscresson.org/pray-with-saint-francis/.

Action Step

PRAY THROUGH THE peace prayer above and take some time to reflect on where peace is needed in your relationships. Pray especially about whether God is inviting you to play a role in healing broken relationships. If nothing comes to mind, simply reflect on this beautiful prayer using the steps of *lecto divina* from Day 12, but apply them to the peace prayer. What words or phrases stand out to you? What does God want to say to you? How are you responding? Use the space below to journal your experience.

Going Deeper

IF YOU'D LIKE to learn more about St. Francis and how he impacted those around him, check out one of his biographies. I recommend *Saint Francis of Assisi* by G.K. Chesterton or *The Life of St. Francis of Assisi* by St. Bonaventure.

PART 7

Ignatian Spirituality

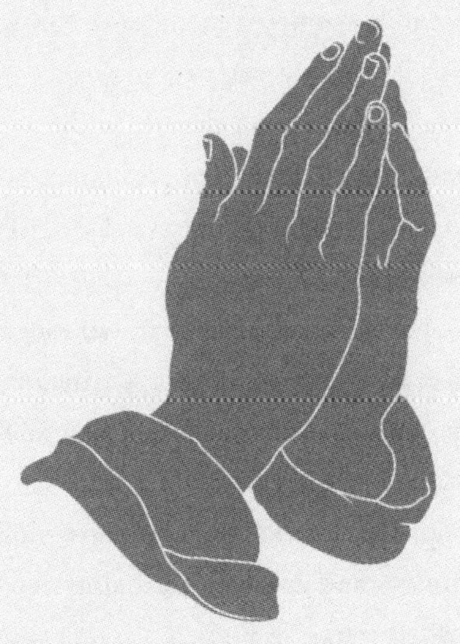

In the early 1500s, a young Spanish knight was struck by a cannonball, which shattered the bones of his leg and changed the world forever. The young knight, Ignatius, had once dreamed of winning glory on the battlefield. With those dreams shattered (along with his leg), Ignatius found himself bedridden for months with nothing to entertain him except books on the lives of the saints and the life of Christ. It was during these months that he experienced a deep conversion of heart and began to long to win glory not for himself on the battlefield but for God. He wanted to become a soldier for Christ.

Ignatius poured his heart into Christian formation and study, became a Catholic priest and theologian, and eventually went on to start a new religious order called the Society of Jesus, known more commonly today as the Jesuits.

A key aspect of becoming a member of the Society of Jesus was undergoing what St. Ignatius referred to as the "Spiritual Exercises," a four-week retreat centered on the unconditional love of God the Father and Christ's mission of redemption. Just as one needs to exercise the body in order to become physically fit, Ignatius argued that one must exercise the soul.

Though the retreat that he wrote lasted four weeks, many of Ignatius's principles and prayer practices are meant to be carried over into daily prayer. These systems of prayer that St. Ignatius developed speak to his brilliance as a spiritual master. Many books have been written about Ignatian spirituality, perhaps more than any other Catholic spirituality, and many great saints have come from the order, spiritual masters like St. Francis Xavier, wonderful theologians like St. Robert Bellarmine, missionary martyrs like St. Isaac Jogues, and other renowned holy men like St. Stanislaus Kostka.

Before going into Ignatian spirituality, we need to spend a brief moment talking about two terms that appear frequently: consolation and desolation. These two terms are fundamental to understanding St. Ignatius's spirituality and the prayer methods we'll be examining.

In the third "Rule of Discernment" from his *Spiritual Exercises,* St. Ignatius gives three descriptions for what he calls consolation:

1. Anything that causes the soul to become "inflamed with the love of her creator."
2. Being moved to tears that lead to deeper love of God.
3. The increase of faith, hope, and love in one's soul, which in turn leads to a greater spiritual joy, attracts us to heavenly things, and instills in us a sense of peacefulness.[29]

In other words, consolation is experiencing the abiding presence of God in our hearts. Sometimes this is an emotional movement of joy or love, or even a type of sadness and sharing in God's suffering. Other times it can be a deep sense of peace and ability to rest in God's presence. At the heart of consolation is the experience of closeness to God.

Desolation, on the other hand, is the opposite of consolation. Whereas in consolation we find an interior peacefulness, in desolation we experience a sort of spiritual restlessness. We are not at peace, and we find ourselves giving in more easily to impatience and unhealthy thought patterns. Whereas we feel drawn toward

[29] St. Ignatius of Loyola, *The Spiritual Exercises of Saint Ignatius* ([1914] Charlotte, NC: TAN Books, 2010), 208.

God in times of consolation, in desolation we feel drawn toward earthly or sinful things.

Now that we have a general understanding of consolation and desolation, we can begin to look more deeply at Ignatius's methods of prayer. On the first day, we look at St. Ignatius's imaginative method for praying with Scripture. On the second day we consider Ignatius's principle daily spiritual practice: the Examen. Finally, on the third day we investigate how we can discern God's will for our lives using St. Ignatius's rules for discernment.

Day 23

Imaginative Prayer with Scripture

ONE OF THE greatest spiritual insights that St. Ignatius discovered was the ability of the Holy Spirit to speak to us through our imaginations. When we hear the word "imagination," we often think of creating stories, but what St. Ignatius really means is the ability of our mind to picture things — for example, we can close our eyes and picture ourselves back in our childhood home, we can mentally relive our memories, and we can enter into a great story that we are reading.

St. Ignatius taught that just as the Holy Spirit can inspire our hearts and our minds, he can speak to us through mental images in our imaginations as well, especially when we use our imaginations to enter into Scripture passages. The Ignatian model of praying with Scripture involves reading a passage and then allowing our imaginations to paint a picture of what is taking place so that the passage can more deeply penetrate our hearts as we visualize what is happening and Jesus can speak to us in a more personal way.

As you read a Scripture passage in this imaginative, Ignatian way, you'll want to pay attention to details. Try to make the experience as vivid as possible, engaging all of your senses: sight, sound, taste, smell, touch. The goal is to insert yourself into the story as much as you are able. Familiarize yourself with the passage, then allow it to unfold in your imagination.

Once you get the hang of visualizing and inserting yourself into the passage, you want to start paying attention. Where are you located in the story? Are you a bystander, one of the disciples, a key character, or someone else? What are the others' facial expressions? What thoughts or emotions come to your mind and heart as everything plays out before you? Do you experience any moments of consolation or desolation?

For some people, this type of prayer is more difficult than others. Some of us are naturally more visual than others and will have no trouble entering into this imaginative meditation, but others will struggle with visualizing details. Don't get too caught up in any expectations; pray for the Holy Spirit to enlighten your imagination and guide your prayer. If you find yourself not really caring for it, I encourage you to come back and try it again someday with an open mind. You never know — the Lord could one day choose to speak to your heart in a powerful way through this technique. For today, give it a shot and see how it goes.

✎ Action Step ✎

TODAY YOU WILL try to pray through a Scripture passage using St. Ignatius's imaginative prayer technique. Here are the steps to get you started. Use the space provided to write about your experience.

1. Take a few moments and try to clear your mind of any distractions. Breathe in and out deeply, and recognize that you are in the presence of God. He is gazing at you with love and wants to speak to you.
2. Read the passage you have chosen once or twice to get an idea of what happens in the passage. For this first initial practice, we will use Luke 5:1–11 (RSVCE):

While the people pressed upon him to hear the word of God, he was standing by the lake of Gennes'aret. And he saw two boats by the lake; but the fishermen had gone out of them and were washing their nets. Getting into one of the boats, which was Simon's, he asked him to put out a little from the land. And he sat down and taught the people from the boat. And when he had ceased speaking, he said to Simon, "Put out into the deep and let down your nets for a catch." And Simon answered, "Master, we toiled all night and took nothing! But at your word I will let down the nets." And when they had done this, they enclosed a great shoal of fish; and as their nets were breaking, they beckoned to their partners in the other boat to come and help them. And they came and filled both the boats, so that they began to sink. But when Simon Peter saw it, he fell down at Jesus' knees, saying, "Depart from me, for I am a sinful man, O Lord." For he was astonished, and all that were with him, at the catch of fish which they had taken; and so also were James and John, sons of Zeb'edee, who were partners with Simon. And Jesus said to Simon, "Do not be afraid; henceforth you will be catching men." And when they had brought their boats to land, they left everything and followed him.

1. Now, close your eyes and try to imagine the setting. Try to engage all five of your senses. What do you see? Hear? Taste? Smell? Feel? In your imagination, picture yourself there in the scene.

2. Say a quick prayer to the Holy Spirit, giving permission to God to speak to you through your imagination. Read the passage again and place yourself in the scene. This time, allow your imagination to wander. What do you see taking place? What thoughts and feelings are going through your mind and heart? Feel free to walk about and talk to Jesus or one of the other people present in the reading. What do you say? What do they say in return? Do not be concerned about historical accuracy, but allow God to speak to you freely in your imagination as the story unfolds. Anything can happen.

3. Do this as often as you'd like, going back to the same scene and meeting Jesus or the other biblical characters there. Are they saying something to you with their words or actions, or perhaps even in their facial expressions? Pay close attention to the movements in your heart — especially for moments of consolation.

In the space below, write about your experience with this exercise.

____

____

____

____

Going Deeper

THE BOOK *An Ignatian Introduction to Prayer: Scriptural Reflections according to the Spiritual Exercises* by Fr. Timothy Gallagher is filled with wonderful examples of imaginative prayer exercises. It is the best place to start if you want to learn more about this prayer method.

Day 24

The Daily Examen

JUST AS WE use the gift of our imagination to reflect and enter more deeply into Scripture, we can also use it to reflect on our lives as we allow God to speak to us. St. Ignatius called the practice of reflecting back on our day in this manner the "Examen." This simple yet profound Examen was so fundamental to his spiritual practice that he instructed members of his order to do it twice a day, which is still required of Jesuits today at noon and at the end of the day.

The Examen is similar to the examination of conscience that we explored in Day 4, and the two are often mistakenly confused as being the same thing. However, there are some key differences. The biggest of these is that the primary focus in the examination of conscience is bringing our sins into the light so that we don't leave anything out when we go to confess them. In the Examen, the focus is more on what has been going on in our hearts throughout the day. The Examen is simply taking a few moments to enter into a conversation with God to take a look at how your relationship with Him is going. It emphasizes finding those things that have been leading you closer to Him and rooting out the things that have been leading you away from Him so that you can experience deep intimacy with God and grow in holiness.

There are four steps to making the Examen:[30]

[30] St. Ignatius of Loyola, *The Spiritual Exercises of Saint Ignatius*, 202.

1. Begin by thanking God for the many blessings He has bestowed upon you.

2. Ask the Holy Spirit to help you know your faults and correct them.

3. Reflect on the past day (or however long it's been since your last Examen) and enter into a dialogue with God, recognizing the ways that you have sinned and what led to that point. Pay particular attention to where you felt God's presence (consolation), and what led you away from Him.

4. Repent and ask God to pardon you from your sins and help you in the future.

Some followers of St. Ignatius recommend a fifth step of looking ahead and making resolutions to avoid falling in the same manner.

✎ Action Step ✎

AT THE END of the day today, try making a daily Examen. You can use the reflection questions and space below to help.

- **Thanksgiving** — What are you most grateful for today? How have you experienced God's love?

- **Prayer for Self-Knowledge** — Ask God to enlighten your mind and enflame your heart as you begin to review the day.
- **Reflect** — Where did you experience consolation today? Where did you experience desolation today?

- **Ask for Forgiveness** — Where do you need the Lord's mercy and healing today? What are the opportunities for moral growth that God brought to your attention during your review?

____

____

____

____

- **Resolutions** — What are some concrete ways you can take what you learned tonight and apply it to tomorrow? What are the times and places where you think you will need God's help the most? What can you do to prepare yourself?

____

____

____

____

Going Deeper

IF YOU WANT to learn more about the daily Examen, there are two books I recommend:

- *The Examen Prayer: Ignatian Wisdom for Our Lives Today* by Timothy Gallagher
- *In His Spirit: A Guide to Today's Spirituality* by Fr. Richard Hauser

Day 25

Discerning God's Will for Your Life

ON OUR FINAL day with Ignatian spirituality, we take a brief look at St. Ignatius's "14 Rules for Discernment." These rules are designed to help us become more aware of what is taking place in our souls. In a nutshell, living out these rules is a sure way that we can train ourselves to listen to the voice of God.

A complete text of the rules can be found in Appendix D, but to keep things simple (and easy to manage in one sitting), I've condensed the rules here to a set of guidelines for recognizing the voice of God, as opposed to our own inner voice or the voice of the evil one.

1. When we are caught in a cycle of sin, the evil one tries to keep us distracted by continuing to suggest new vices. God, on the other hand, tries to snap us out of it by poking our conscience.

2. When we strive to break out of a cycle of sin and vice, the evil one throws obstacles in our way, trying to make us feel uneasy by feeding us lies that make our task seem impossible. God, on the other hand, is the voice of encouragement and strength.

3. Consolation and desolation can help us find the movement of God. Remember that consolation is an experience of interior peace and resting in God's presence, and desolation is a state of spiritual agitation and restlessness.

4. If we resolve to do something while in a state of consolation, we should continue to carry through with it, *even when we begin to experience desolation*. When we are in consolation, we are being guided and counseled by the good spirit, but when we are in desolation we are receiving counsel from the bad spirit.

5. There are three reasons for spiritual desolation: (a) We have grown lazy in spiritual things, and God withdraws the experience of His presence to help us recognize it before we fall into serious sin. (b) God is allowing us to grow spiritually and seek to do what is right for God's sake and not for the purpose of experiencing consoling feelings. (c) God is helping us grow in humility and recognize that every good thing is from God and we can do nothing on our own.

6. When we find ourselves in spiritual desolation, we should fight against it by doubling down on our prayer efforts, especially if the cause of the desolation is spiritual laziness. No matter what, trust that God is there, even if you can't feel His presence, and know that you will experience consolation again soon.

7. When we are in consolation, we should remember that it is a gift and that we can very well find ourselves in desolation again. In both consolation and desolation, we should remember that our strength comes from the Lord.

8. Be aware that you have an enemy who hates you. The devil will try to throw temptations at you when you

strive to grow closer to God. He will attack at your weakest points — tempting you to the vices to which you are most prone. Don't give the enemy any leeway — little moral failures lead to big moral failures.

9. The enemy wants to remain in the shadows. Temptations spoken aloud vanish like smoke. Satan doesn't want you to be aware that he is the one trying to trap you and lead you away from God. When we are feeling tempted, we should acknowledge it and bring it into the light. This is another reason why both the Examen and the Sacrament of Reconciliation are such powerful tools for conquering sin in our lives.

✎ Action Step ✎

FOR TODAY'S ACTION step, I'd like you to read through these guidelines again, but this time take time to try and think of moments in your life where you've experienced the truth of each of these steps in some way. Use these questions as a means of reflecting on these guidelines.

1. Have you ever been caught in a cycle of sin, consciously or unconsciously? How did you feel spiritually? Can you recall a moment where God poked your conscience or tried to snap you out of it?

____

____

____

____

2. Can you recall a time in your life where you tried to break a vice or habitual sin? What were some lies the evil one used to make you feel like it was impossible? How did God encourage you?

____

____

____

____

3. Can you think of when you have resolved to do something good and felt completely at peace with it—only to feel anxious or restless the next day?

4. Would you say you are currently in a state of consolation or desolation? If desolation, what do you believe is its cause? Based on these guidelines, what should you do to respond?

5. Where does the devil attack you most frequently? What temptations does he throw your way? Combat them by bringing them into the light.

Going Deeper

I RECOMMEND THREE books for those looking to learn more about St. Ignatius's Rules for Discernment and for making big decisions in life:

- *The Discernment of Spirits: An Ignatian Guide for Everyday Living* by Fr. Timothy Gallagher
- *Discerning the Will of God: The Ignatian Guide for Christian Decision Making* by Fr. Timothy Gallagher
- *True North: A Roadmap for Discernment* by Joel Stepanek

PART 8

Dominican Spirituality

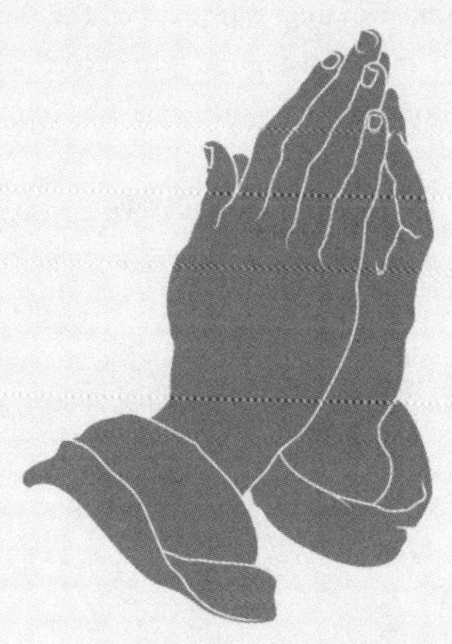

St. Dominic, one of the most revered saints in human history, was born in the late 1100s in a small town in Spain. He began as a priest of the Benedictine order, but he eventually founded his own religious order. Though today we know them as Dominicans, the true name of St. Dominic's order is the Order of Preachers.

There are four main pillars of the Dominican order: prayer, study, community, and service. Dominican service often takes the form of preaching and teaching. Like the Franciscans, the Dominicans were supported only through almsgiving, and they traveled the countryside preaching the gospel. They also developed a revolutionary educational system and were committed to teaching others the Catholic Faith.

St. Dominic's entire life was a model of faith, prayer, and action. One day, while St. Dominic was praying, the Blessed Virgin Mary appeared to him and taught him the Rosary! This devotion spread like wildfire throughout the medieval Church, and it became a source of great devotion and renewal.[31]

To this day, Dominicans are especially well known for their contribution to the study of theology. In fact, though all of the religious orders have produced their fair share of theologians, the Dominicans in particular seem to be a sort of factory for them. The great Dominican St. Thomas Aquinas, who is considered one of the greatest minds who ever lived, has an entire theological/philosophical school of thought called Thomism, which really laid the foundation for theological studies in the West.

[31] We look more closely at the rosary on Day 37.

Theology seeks to more deeply comprehend what God has revealed. Unlike the empirical sciences, theology is not the study of observable phenomena in the natural world. Rather, theology looks at what God has revealed about Himself to man. It is "faith seeking understanding," to quote St. Anselm. The empirical sciences answer the big questions of *what* and *how*. Theology, in a sense more akin to philosophy, answers the questions of *who* and *why*.

Over the next few days, we will look especially at prayer through the lenses of studying and evangelization by teaching, two major elements of Dominican spirituality. As we focus on these methods of prayer, we ask, St. Dominic, pray for us!

Day 26

Studying Scripture

As we addressed early on our journey, reading the Bible is an essential part of the journey of discipleship. So far, we've prayerfully engaged with the Word through *lectio divina* and explored how to enter more deeply into passages through Ignatian imaginative prayer. Today we look at what it means to actually *study* Sacred Scripture.

Understanding Sacred Scripture is not always easy, but as we meditate on what it means to have "faith seeking understanding" in the light of Dominican spirituality, there is no better way to pursue God's truth than through the study of His written Word. Unfortunately, many theologians, especially in the modern age, have fallen into the trap of reducing the study of Scripture to simply an intellectual exercise, rather than a movement from faith seeking to learn more. Though Scripture study certainly requires intellectual exercise and using the full capacity of our minds, it truly ought to be a movement of the heart. Most importantly, Scripture study should never be separated from a spirit of prayer. There is a saying in the Church that "theology is done best on one's knees"—we must remain humble and prayerful whenever we approach the Lord to understand more about Him. For St. Dominic and his followers, the intellectual pursuit of God's truth was always about coming to know and love God more and teaching others about Him.

The Church gives us three key principles for interpreting Scripture passages that we should always keep in mind:

1. We need to be attentive to "the content and unity of the whole Scripture."[32] In other words, we can't just read one passage and interpret it outside of its context. This helps prevent the weaponization of Scripture passages used to push certain agendas. We need to keep in mind the whole content and unity of what God has spoken through His Word.

2. We need to read Scripture from within the "living Tradition of the whole Church."[33] The Church and Scripture go hand in hand. The Church gave us Scripture and decided which books were to be included and which books were excluded. We therefore shouldn't try to separate the Bible from the living memory of the Church. The Church's interpretation of Scripture is the definitive interpretation when it comes to defining doctrinal matters.

3. We have to keep in mind the "analogy of faith" (CCC 114). This is the idea that there is an inner coherence among matters of Faith, and God doesn't contradict himself. Anything appearing to be a contradiction in Scripture is in reality an invitation to deeper reflection on who God is and what He is revealing to us.

In addition to these three principles, the *Catechism* also speaks of two "senses" of Scripture; the *literal sense* and the *spiritual sense* (CCC 115). The *literal* sense of Scripture can be summarized as the meaning

[32] Vatican Council II, Dogmatic Constitution on Divine Revelation *Dei verbum*, no. 12.

[33] Vatican Council II, Dogmatic Constitution on Divine Revelation *Dei verbum*, no. 12.

of the written words, or what the human author meant in their writing. Understand that we are not supposed to take every Scripture passage literally. Many parts of Scripture use common literary genres of their time, including poetry and metaphorical language. Scripture scholars therefore study the culture and language of the ancient texts in order to help us have a clear understanding of what the text actually is meant to say — this is the true meaning of "literal sense." For example, the Church does not teach that we need to believe from the Creation account in Genesis 1–2 that the universe was literally created in seven days, but we do need to understand from it that God created an ordered universe and that He created it to be good. This is what we mean when we are talking about interpreting the literal sense of a passage.

Because Scripture is truly the word of God, there is also a *spiritual* sense to understanding Scripture — a deeper spiritual meaning that God reveals to us through the text. Just as a great author includes foreshadowing in his or her stories, God uses events in human history to foreshadow His work of salvation.

This spiritual sense is traditionally broken into three subdivisions: the allegorical, the moral, and the anagogical. The *allegorical sense* refers to how all Scripture points to Christ in some way. For example, the manna in the desert is a foreshadowing of the Eucharist, and the binding of Isaac by Abraham is a foreshadowing of Jesus' sacrifice on the Cross. The *moral sense* of Scripture refers to portions of Scripture that teach us how to live our lives in an upright manner. This happens either directly, as in the exhortations by Jesus and St. Paul in the New Testament, or indirectly, such as when Scripture gives us models of how we should or shouldn't act through the actions of characters in the Bible. Finally, the anagogical sense refers to viewing the passage through the lens of our eternity. We understand the events and passages in light of their eternal significance, allowing our hearts to move toward a deeper longing for God's kingdom to manifest itself in our hearts and in the world.

As St. Augustine famously wrote, the New Testament is "hidden" in the Old and the Old Testament is "revealed" in the New. Though the Bible is made up of seventy-three different books, there is a wonderful cohesiveness to it. Take time to read it and pray with it, but also take time to study it. Look for the connections and the way that everything ties together. Allow the Holy Spirit to move both your heart and your mind. This is a sure way to work with grace and grow in faith.

Action Step

TODAY WE'RE GOING to do an exercise in studying Scripture. Remember, just like every form of prayer in this book, this type of reflection will come more easily to some people and others will struggle with it. Don't fret if this is difficult for you. It speaks to the fact that each of us has unique gifts and talents and ways that we connect with God!

Prayerfully read and reread the following passage from the book of Ezekiel, then use the reflection questions to practice studying Scripture.

> The hand of the LORD was upon me, and he brought me out by the Spirit of the LORD, and set me down in the midst of the valley; it was full of bones. And he led me round among them; and behold, there were very many upon the valley; and lo, they were very dry. And he said to me, "Son of man, can these bones live?" And I answered, "O Lord GOD, thou knowest." Again he said to me, "Prophesy to these bones, and say to them, O dry bones, hear the word of the LORD. Thus says the Lord GOD to these bones: Behold, I will cause breath to enter you, and you shall live. And I will lay sinews upon you, and will cause flesh to come upon you, and cover you with skin, and put breath in you, and you shall live; and you shall know that I am the LORD."
>
> So I prophesied as I was commanded; and as I prophesied, there was a noise, and behold, a rattling; and the bones came together, bone to its bone. And as I looked, there were sinews on them, and flesh had come upon them, and skin had covered them; but there was no breath in them. Then he said to me, "Prophesy to the breath, prophesy, son of man, and say to the breath, Thus says the Lord GOD: Come from the four winds, O breath, and breathe upon these

slain, that they may live." So I prophesied as he commanded me, and the breath came into them, and they lived, and stood upon their feet, an exceedingly great host.

Then he said to me, "Son of man, these bones are the whole house of Israel. Behold, they say, 'Our bones are dried up, and our hope is lost; we are clean cut off.' Therefore prophesy, and say to them, Thus says the Lord God: Behold, I will open your graves, and raise you from your graves, O my people; and I will bring you home into the land of Israel. And you shall know that I am the Lord, when I open your graves, and raise you from your graves, O my people. And I will put my Spirit within you, and you shall live, and I will place you in your own land; then you shall know that I, the Lord, have spoken, and I have done it, says the Lord." (Ezek. 37:1–14, RSVCE)

1. This text recounts a vision experienced by the prophet Ezekiel in the sixth century B.C., when the Jewish people were in exile in Babylon. What is the literal meaning of the text? In your own words, what did the sacred author want to communicate to the person reading or listening to the passage?

2. How does this passage connect to Jesus' mission or the mission of the Holy Spirit? Are there any significant moments in the New Testament that this passage seems to foreshadow?

3. As you read, do you sense any call to action that God has for you? What is the eternal significance of the passage? What is God promising here? What does He want us to know about our eternal significance or destiny?

Going Deeper

In addition to the Going Deeper resources listed for Day 6, I recommend the following:

- *New Testament Basics for Catholics* by John Bergsma
- *Psalm Basics for Catholics: Seeing Salvation History in a New Way* by John Bergsma
- *Love Basics for Catholics: Illustrating God's Love for Us throughout Scripture* by John Bergsma

There are also some great Bible study resources out there. Here are a few that stand out:

- The *Journey through Scripture* Bible Studies by the St. Paul Center for Biblical Theology (found at stpaulcenter.com/bible-studies)
- *The Great Adventure: Your Journey through the Bible* by Ascension Press

As always, these lists are not exhaustive but are meant to be a good starting place for you.

Day 27

Teaching the Faith to Others

ONE OF THE key pieces of Dominican spirituality is teaching others. After all, the Dominicans are called the Order of Preachers for a reason! People are often drawn to the Dominican order if they enjoy philosophical and theological discussion and love to share with others in a teaching or preaching setting the wonders of the mystery of God.

Teaching the Faith is not like teaching any other subject. In order to pass the Faith on to others, we ourselves must be people of faith and deep prayer. The Catholic Faith is something that engages the entire person: both the mind *and* heart need to be fed. To neglect either formational aspect would be a disservice to those being taught. If you are in a position of handing on this sacred Faith to others, you *must* be spending time in prayer. There is simply no way to be successful in ministry if we are not taking our prayer lives seriously. This isn't important only for the sake of those we are teaching, but it is critical for our own spiritual health as well. Unfortunately, ministry workers sometimes burn out and grow bitter toward the Church or even leave the Church altogether. The root of this failure is that these people are almost always trying to do ministry by relying on their own strength alone, and they do not take the time to be *filled* by their faith. The best advice I ever received in ministry was incredibly simple: "Stay prayed up." As Jesus said,

> Abide in me, and I in you. As the branch cannot bear fruit by itself, unless it abides in the vine, neither can you, unless you abide in me. I am the vine, you are the branches. He who abides in me, and I in him, he it is that bears much fruit, for apart from me you can do nothing. (John 15:4–5, RSVCE)

Indeed, by taking time to abide in prayer, God can do wonderful things in and through you.

St. Bernard wrote about the importance of being filled with the Holy Spirit — and not just a channel for him — in his work *On the Song of Songs*:

> Those who are wise will see their lives as more like a reservoir than a canal. The canal simultaneously pours out what it receives; the reservoir retains the water till it is filled, then pours forth the overflow without loss to itself. . . . Today there are many in the Church who act like canals, the reservoirs are far too rare. So urgent is the charity of those through whom the streams of heavenly doctrine flow to us that they want to pour it forth before they have been filled. They are more ready to speak than to listen, impatient to teach what they have not yet grasped, and full of presumption to govern others while they know not how to govern themselves. . . .
>
> The reservoir resembles the fountain that runs to form a stream or spreads to form a pool only when its waters are brimming over. . . . You must imitate this process. First, be filled, and then control the outpouring. The charity that is benign and prudent does not flow outward until it abounds within.[34]

[34] St. Bernard, *On the Song of Songs,* Etext arranged by Darrell Wright, 2008, https://ia800702.us.archive.org/11/items/St.BernardOnTheSongOfSongs/StBernardOnTheSongOfSongsall.wps.pdf, sermon 18, paras. 3 and 4.

In other words, don't just become a canal for the Holy Spirit to move through, become a reservoir!

When you begin to be filled with the Holy Spirit in prayer and share your faith in a teaching role, you'll also find immense growth in your own faith journey. The analogy I like to use to demonstrate this idea is the Sea of Galilee and the Dead Sea. If you look at these two bodies of water on a geographical map, you will see that the Jordan River flows into the Sea of Galilee, but more importantly, it also flows out from the Sea of Galilee. This outflow of the Jordan carries sediment from the sea, and the movement of the water keeps things moving and fresh, so there is great life to be found in the Sea of Galilee. In the Dead Sea, however, there is no outflow. The water flows into it and stops. Because of this, salt and sediment build up and choke all life.

In a similar manner, when we pour out what we receive from God by leading and instructing others in the Faith, new life seems to spring up from within us. The process of learning to teach is just as instructive for our own minds to comprehend the Faith in a deeper way. But if we don't share the Faith with others, things can grow stagnant in our own hearts and minds. We have to use what we are given to build the kingdom. We need to find ways to share the gospel with others if we want to fan the flames of divine life within our souls. We need to teach others about the Faith.

Action Step

Your action step this week is twofold. If you are in a paid or volunteer position that is responsible for teaching others the Catholic Faith, take some time in prayer to reflect on your personal relationship with Jesus. Where is there room for growth? If you are not currently in a position like this, take some time to discern whether this is something you are called to. The Church is always in need of great catechists and ministry workers. Consider talking to the folks at your local parish and getting involved. It could be a great way to grow in your faith as you help stir the flames of faith in others. If you feel called to pursue this ministry path, I invite you to use the space below to write out some action steps you can take or people you need to contact to get involved. You could also use it to write out some of the things that excite you about this possibility or some of the doubts or concerns you may have.

____

____

____

Going Deeper

The most important book that a catechist should familiarize themselves with — aside from the Bible — is the *Catechism of the Catholic Church*. The *Directory of Catechesis* and *Catechesi Tradendae* are also important works that should be studied by anyone in a faith formation director type of role. The most important thing, however, is to continue to abide with Christ in prayer and always be learning more about our Faith.

PART 9

Eastern Catholicism

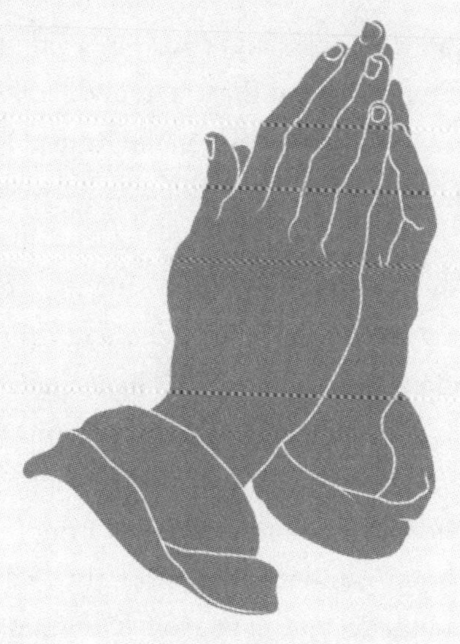

ONE OF THE most beautiful things about our Catholic Faith is the fact that it allows for such a wide range of cultural and spiritual traditions. There are so many different flavors of our Faith. Though we are in union with each other, we are not forced into uniformity. Indeed, the Church respects and even celebrates the vast cultural differences that exist within the different parts of the world.

It surprises some people to hear that even within the Catholic Church there are not only different spiritualities but different "Churches," or rites. Most of us in the western world grew up in the Roman Catholic Rite. However, there are also twenty-three Eastern Catholic rites, such as Byzantine Catholic, Ukrainian Catholic, Maronite Catholic, Melkite Catholic, and Chaldean Catholic. These rites are in communion with Rome, which means that they accept the supremacy of the Pope, we all share in the same sacraments, and we all share the same holy, catholic, and apostolic Faith. However, the way Eastern Rite Catholics live out their faith in their liturgical and prayer practices is different from how folks in the Roman Rite do.

On the surface, some of the differences between the various rites may seem pretty big. For example, in the East married men are allowed to become priests, and when infants are baptized in the Eastern rites, they also receive the Sacraments of Confirmation and First Communion at the same time! The eucharistic celebration in the Eastern Rites is also called Divine Liturgy instead of Holy Mass. The prayers, hymns, and traditions of this liturgy differ from those found in the Roman Mass, but the Divine Liturgy still features Scripture readings, a homily, and most importantly, a valid consecration of the Eucharist and the reception of Holy Communion.

Both Western and Eastern Catholicism have a rich history of spiritual traditions and practices that go back over a millennium, and we can learn so much from each other. In fact, Pope St. John Paul II referred to Eastern and Western Christianity as the "two lungs" of the Church, and he called for the Church to breathe with them both.[35]

Unlike the other sections of this book, which simply focus on different spiritual movements, this section shares two prayer techniques that come from the Eastern Catholic Tradition. If you want to learn more about Eastern Catholicism, I highly suggest seeing if there is an Eastern Catholic church near you and stopping by for a visit. Note, however, that the Eastern Orthodox Church is *not* in communion with Rome; Eastern Catholic churches bear the word "Catholic" in their name.[36] There are also some great videos on YouTube about Eastern Catholicism, especially on the channels *Pints with Aquinas* (by Matt Fradd) and the *Our Lady of Perpetual Help NM* channel.

[35] John Paul II, encyclical letter *Ut Unum Sint* (That They May Be One) (May 25, 1995), https://www.vatican.va/content/john-paul-ii/en/encyclicals/documents/hf_jp-ii_enc_25051995_ut-unum-sint.html.

[36] For a complete list of all Catholic rites that are in full communion with the Church, please see Nicholas LaBanca, "The Other 23 Catholic Churches (Rites) and Why They Exist," Ascension Press, January 21, 2019, https://media.ascensionpress.com/2019/01/21/the-other-23-catholic-churches-and-why-they-exist/.

Day 28

The Jesus Prayer

THE JESUS PRAYER traces its roots all the way back to the sixth century. The words of the prayer are simple, in their fullest form: "Lord Jesus Christ, son of the living God, have mercy on me a sinner." One may also simply pray the name of Jesus or say, "Jesus, have mercy on me," as the vocal prayer for this devotion. It is short and sweet, but it is meant to be repeated for some time. As with all other prayer, we should strive with all of our might to engage our hearts in addition to our minds as we pray.

There are many different ways we can pray this prayer, but the ultimate goal is to sanctify daily life and use it as a means of "praying without ceasing" (1 Thess. 5:17, NABRE). Many spiritual writers recommend praying it for a set amount of time and syncing the prayer to your breathing. For example, as you slowly breathe in you say, "Lord Jesus Christ, son of the living God," and as you breathe out you pray, "Have mercy on me a sinner." By taking five to ten minutes to pray this way, our own breathing becomes a sort of prayer, and we can easily find ourselves entering back into this prayer throughout the day, even in the most mundane places!

Remember, because we are body and soul, it is important to try to involve our senses in prayer, which is why we use incense, sacred art, and bells. Similarly, to help engage the sense of touch, some practitioners of the Jesus Prayer also use a prayer rope called a *chotki*. It is similar to rosary beads, but all the beads are in one set, not arranged in decades. However, it is also perfectly fine to pray this method of prayer without *chotki*. As you pray, don't worry so much about counting how many times you pray the prayer, but rather think of a certain amount of time that you'd like to pray for, or simply pray until you feel you are in a place of contemplation, where your words seem to go silent and heart speaks to Heart. Feel free to come back to the words whenever you need them to lead you back into the heights of contemplation.

Think of how many times throughout the day we are waiting for something to happen — stoplights to turn green, friends to respond to our message, eyes to grow tired. And with modern technology, it is so easy to fill the little in-between moments of life with social media scrolling or playing games on our phones. But imagine how much healthier our society would be if everyone simply traded some of that time to slow down, be present to God and themselves, and breathe and pray this simple prayer. Once you get the hang of it, and begin to find yourself praying this way throughout the day, you'll see what an incredible difference this little prayer can make in your life.

✎ Action Step ✎

PRAY THE JESUS Prayer! Everything you need can be found above. Set aside some time to try it without distractions, and then come back to it from time to time throughout the day. Use the space below to write some notes about the experience.

___

___

___

___

___

___

___

Going Deeper

TO TAKE THE Jesus Prayer a step further, I recommend connecting it with certain routines that you already do. For example, maybe on the drive to work or whenever you do the dishes, you could incorporate this method of prayer. I would recommend reading a book called *The Way of a Pilgrim* if you want to learn more about this method. Though the author is unknown and it comes from the Russian Orthodox Tradition, it is an excellent account of the power of this method of prayer.

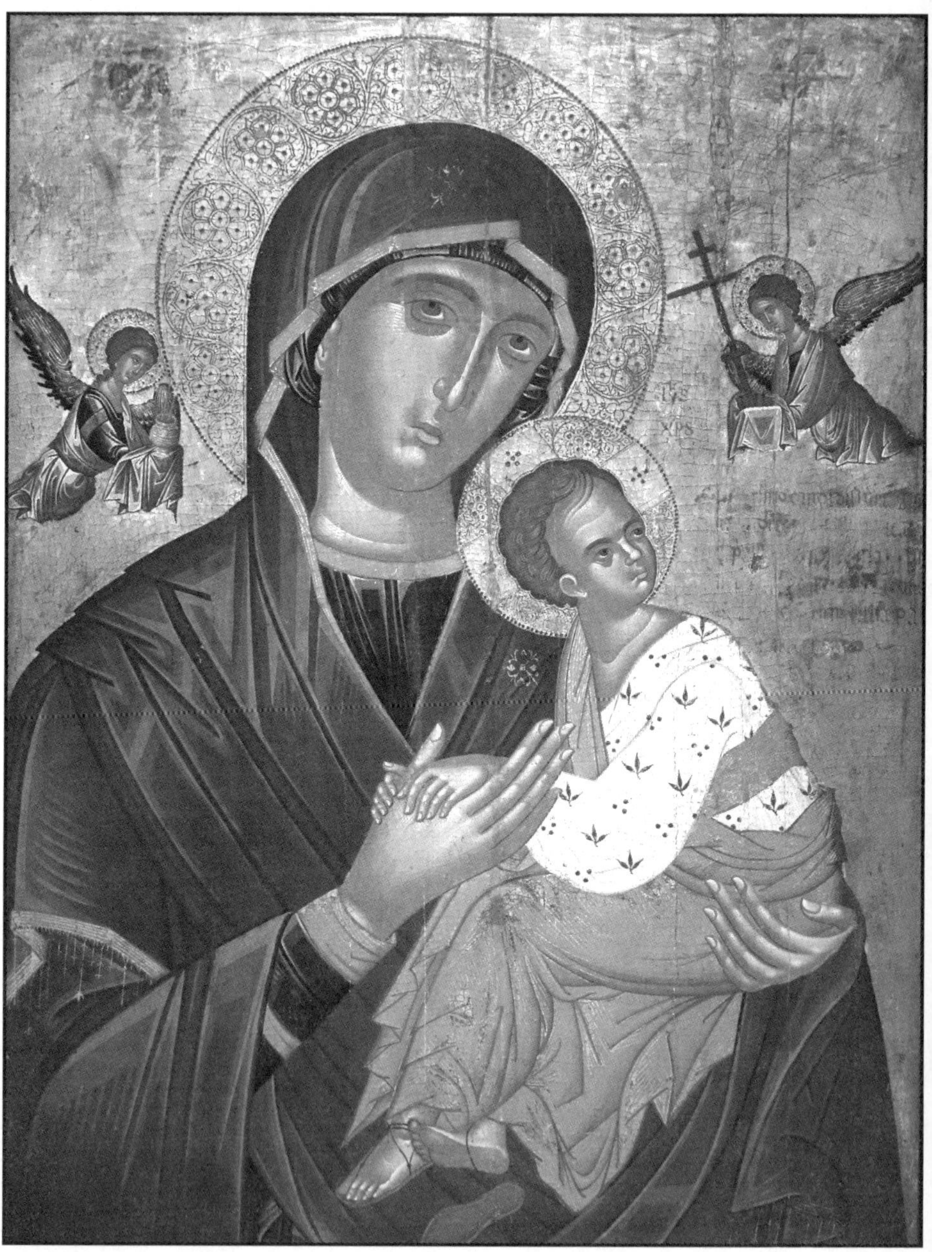

Day 29

Praying with an Icon

ICONS HAVE BEEN a part of the Church since its earliest days. Tradition even suggests that St. Luke the evangelist, the Gospel writer and acquaintance of St. Paul, was the very first iconographer, and legend has it that several icons that have survived to the present day, such as the icon of Our Lady of Czestochowa in Poland, were first painted, or "written," by him.

In a particular way, faithful Christians in the Eastern Roman, or Byzantine, Empire used icons as a tool for devotion and prayer. While iconoclast factions sometimes (and briefly) arose in the East that thought venerating icons was a form of idolatry, on the whole, Eastern Christians have mostly viewed icons as a beautiful means of meditating upon the lives of Christ, the Blessed Virgin Mary, and many other saints, and the promises of Heaven. As always, when we venerate an icon, we do not worship the image itself or the saints it portrays, but we do use the icon to allow our eyes to reflect and contemplate the heavenly image, and we ask the saints for their prayers as we look to their lives as a model and inspiration for following Christ.

You may be surprised to learn that creating an icon is a painstaking process, being both intellectually challenging and labor intensive. The process begins with a wooden board called an "ark" and a special piece of cheesecloth that is used to paint the primer. The drawing is then etched onto the ark and sanded and polished. Following this, the writer places twenty-four-carat gold leaf to it one small piece at a time, and they breathe on it to help it set (which also symbolically represents God "breathing" the Holy Spirit). Special paint is then made from egg emulsions and pigments and applied. Traditionally, icons would contain twenty to thirty layers of paint because they had to be durable to be used in liturgical processions and venerated over and over again by faithful Christians. For the writer of the icon, the process of creating an icon is also one of prayer — representing one's journey toward perfection and growth in holiness. Not only does this work engage the hands and heart, it also fully engages the mind! Iconography has its own set of traditions and symbols that goes back to the earliest days of the Church. Learning these symbols and traditions, and how to build upon them in an organic way, is the task of every iconographer.

Just as icons are written instead of painted, we "read" icons instead of looking at them. Icons are purposefully not photorealistic art pieces, but rather use artistic expression to teach deeper truths than a literal or realistic art piece could. When praying with an icon, it helps to remember that every little detail we see has a deeper meaning behind it. Many times, for example, figures are arranged into geometric patterns to teach an important theological lesson, such as in the famous Rublev Trinity icon, which places the angelic visitors to Abraham in a triangle in order to represent the Holy Trinity and the role of God the Father in Eastern Christianity. One of my favorite examples of this symbolism can be found in the icon *Our Lady of Perpetual Help,* which comes to us from the fifteenth century. If you undertake a close reading, you'll see that one of Jesus' sandals is falling off, which seems strange. The sandal falling off shows Jesus' dependence on His human mother while He lived on earth. It represents that Jesus, moments before, was running into the arms of His mother so quickly that His sandal was falling off. Mary, as Jesus' mother, was a refuge and sanctuary for Him, and she wants to be that for us as well. What a beautiful reflection for us to ponder. Icons often direct us to turn to Scripture or the Traditions of the Church as we seek to understand the story and message they are telling. In this way, icons are as much theological tools for teaching as they are means of prayer and meditation.

One popular way of praying with icons is to apply the rules for *lectio divina* to your reflection. First, quiet your heart and spend some time simply gazing upon the icon. What strikes your eye? Then begin a conversation with God about the icon: ask questions and listen for answers, or write them down so that you can seek the answers later. Pay attention to the interior movements in your soul: What emotions or thoughts are stirring? Finally, take some time in silence to contemplate God's mystery and rest in His presence.

✎ Action Step ✎

TRY TO PRAY with an icon today. Take time to quiet your heart and remove any distractions before you begin. For your convenience, we've included an image of the icon of Our Lady of Perpetual Help, one of my absolute favorites. Take note of any little details that catch your eye. As you meditate on the image, remember that icons are a window into Heaven. Allow yourself to feel and encounter the presence of the living God. Use the space below to journal your experience.

____

____

____

____

Going Deeper

IF YOU'D LIKE to learn a little more about the process of creating icons, I encourage you to check out the article "Icons — A Beginner's Guide" by Cheryl Hadley at https://www.catholiccompany.com/magazine/icons-a-beginners-guide. For a deeper dive, see *Sacred Doorways: A Beginner's Guide to Icons* by Linette Martin.

PART 10

Other Forms of Prayer

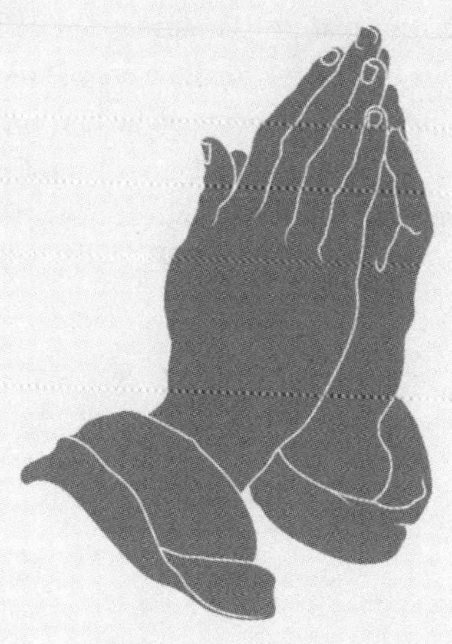

In this section of the book, we look at several other devotions, spiritualities, and methods you can incorporate into your prayer life. So many wonderful ways to pray have been passed down through the Tradition of the Church over the centuries. In the following pages you'll learn about making pilgrimages, the Litany of Humility, prayerfully meditating on death, prayer as a tool for spiritual combat, praying novenas, divine mercy, and praying with the saints. Countless other methods could be placed in this section, but I believe these seven are of particular value in today's world, especially for those who are in the process of deepening their prayer journey for the first time.

As you proceed through this section, I encourage you to do so with an open mind. The titles of some of these prayers may seem strange or foreign at first. In fact, I *hope* that is the case, because that means you have the opportunity to learn something new! It's also worth repeating here that just because a certain method of prayer doesn't seem to be fruitful for you now doesn't mean you won't find it fruitful in the future. What some people find boring or uncomfortable, others find exciting and life-giving, and sometimes prayer methods that we just couldn't get into at one point become our favorite a couple of months or years later.

Day 30

Going on a Pilgrimage

When you hear about "going on a pilgrimage," you most likely think of taking a trip halfway around the world to the Holy Lands, the Camino del Santiago, Fátima, Rome, or another holy site. These are places that have special significance to us as Catholics and are common pilgrimage destinations. As we'll see, however, there are many less recognizable pilgrimage sites; some of them exist in our own local cities and dioceses!

Before plunging into some practical way of incorporating more pilgrimages in your life, it would be beneficial for us to take a look at what a pilgrimage is. Put simply, a pilgrimage is a spiritual journey, most often in the form of a physical journey to a place of religious importance. Many pilgrimages take us to places where Jesus or one of the saints walked, or a place where a Marian apparition occurred. The purpose of a pilgrimage is to grow spiritually; pilgrims often bring a special intention to pray for throughout the journey.

Going on a pilgrimage such as to the Holy Lands, Rome, Assisi, Lourdes, and the like can be an incredibly powerful experience. To walk where Jesus walked, or see the place where St. Paul was martyred or St. Francis preached or the Blessed Mother appeared is a surreal experience. Countless people undergo powerful conversions in their hearts and minds, so much so that we often hear these journeys referred to as a "faith-awakening" experience.

That being said, going on a journey halfway around the world is usually a once-in-a-lifetime opportunity, and for some people it simply isn't an option due to finances or poor health or a fear or distaste for travel. But there are other ways to make a pilgrimage without spending a small fortune or traveling great distances.

You can find smaller shrines and pilgrimage locations in many places throughout the world. Perhaps there is a church close to you that has relics of saints you are devoted to, or maybe a local shrine is devoted to a particular saint with whom you really connect. You can also visit your local cathedral or a place where a local miracle happened or a spot that a certain saint visited. Some of these local pilgrimages may take a day, but many will take just a couple of hours. The point of these pilgrimages is simply to take time to *journey out of the familiar* for a spiritual purpose — to deepen your connection to God. Remember, though, that a pilgrimage isn't a fun day trip or a vacation: these are holy experiences of prayer in order to grow closer to God and to perfect our souls.

If all else fails, a purely spiritual experience of purposely drawing closer to God for a time can also be considered a pilgrimage. The Lenten season is often described as a pilgrimage, and even taking time to work through this book could be considered a sort of spiritual pilgrimage. In fact, our whole Christian life can and should be considered a pilgrimage toward heaven, the final destination toward which we strive and journey together.

✎ Action Step ✎

MAKE A PLAN to go on a pilgrimage sometime in the next year. Though a pilgrimage can be a purely spiritual experience, try to physically get out and travel in some way, even to someplace local. Contact your local diocese and ask about any pilgrimage sites they may recommend, or ask your parish priest about the relics in your parish or other nearby churches. There is something wonderful about being on a physical journey that represents the spiritual journey we are on and reminds us that we are mind, soul, *and* body. Embrace the spirit of adventure and embark on your own personal pilgrimage. Feel free to use the space below to write out your plan for completing this action step, or simply to jot down some ideas for pilgrimages you would like to go on one day.

Going Deeper

For some excellent information about pilgrimages, go to www.catholicshrines.org. You can learn more about the history of pilgrimages and how to make the most of one at the "Making a Pilgrimage" tab on the website. They also have a United States "Shrine Directory" page that is a great tool if you are looking for some ideas of places where you can go on a pilgrimage!

Day 31

Remembering Your Death (*Memento Mori*)

WE CONCLUDED YESTERDAY'S reflection by noting that each of us is on a spiritual journey toward heaven. Today we take that a step further as we explore a tradition that while at first may seem morbid, upon closer review is both beautiful and spiritually liberating. It begins with the recognition of a very simple truth: someday you are going to die.

Recognizing this fact isn't just some sort of thought exercise in existential philosophy; it is a reality that we need to learn to address. Everyone will die, but the thought of our death does not need to lead us to fear and dread. Reflecting on death can actually be a beautiful method of meditative prayer that can help us conquer our fear and grow in greater trust and love of our Creator. In fact, in some medieval monasteries, monks would greet one another with the phrase *Frater, memento mori,* which translates, "Brother, remember your death."

We need to remember our death for two reasons. The first is that our death is when our souls will separate from our bodies, we will encounter God face-to-face, and we will be judged for our lives. When we meditate on our death and judgment, we ought to be strengthened in our resolve to do good and avoid evil. St. Ignatius actually recommended imagining yourself on your deathbed as a means of making quick discernments for choices when you are in a pinch![37] And St. Benedict urged his monks to remind themselves daily that they will one day die.[38] If hindsight is 20-20, imagining how we'd feel about a certain action while on our deathbed or while awaiting God's judgment can help us figure out what we should do in any difficult moment. How do we want to look back on our life and our choices?

The other reason we remember our death is to recall the fact that death has been defeated. We don't need to be afraid of death. It is not the end of our story, but it *is* a crucial part of it. Each of us will experience death, but more importantly, each of us will also experience resurrection — hopefully to new life in Christ, the "firstborn" from the dead (Col. 1:18, NABRE). The Cross of Christ has triumphed, and we follow Jesus through death to life. St. Francis even referred to death as "Sister Death" in his *Canticle of the Sun*, because "those whom death will find in Your most holy will" will find no harm as they pass "from earthly life into the heavenly kingdom." We should therefore think about our death in light of our promised eternal life and meditate on the hope and peace that Christ has promised us. We will one day die, and we don't know the day or hour, but we can rest assured that if we follow Christ throughout our lives, we will experience His incredible peace when we die.

However, if you ever find yourself struggling with the fear of death, turn to St. Joseph, the foster father of Jesus, spouse of Mary, and "patron of a happy death." St. Joseph is believed to have died in the arms of Mary and Jesus, and one could not ask for a more peaceful pair to be with us when we pass. We can always ask Joseph to pray for us if we feel afraid, and we can also ask Mary and Jesus to embrace us in our death as they embraced Joseph in his.

[37] St. Ignatius of Loyola, *The Spiritual Exercises of Saint Ignatius,* 69.

[38] *The Rule of St. Benedict in English,* ch. 4, v. 44.

There are several ways that you can incorporate the idea of *memento mori* into your prayer life. A good place to start may be prayerfully reading and meditating on Psalm 39, which serves as a beautiful reminder from Scripture about our mortality. You could also do as St. Ignatius suggests, using imaginative prayer to picture yourself at the end of your earthly life and allowing that to be a prayerful encounter with God. Another way to pray could be simply reflecting on the question "If I were to die tomorrow, what would I want today to heal my relationship with God and others in my life?" When praying with any of these methods, it's important to reflect on whether God is calling you to a particular action or to make some changes in your life. While the idea of death can sometimes bring up some difficult feelings, invite God into them and offer them as a prayer of sacrifice to God. Ask God to work in your heart, purify your mind, and draw your desires to seek Him and His kingdom above all else.

✎ Action Step ✎

CHOOSE ONE OF the three *memento mori* meditative prayer exercises from above (Scripture reflection, Ignatian imaginative prayer about the hour of death, or reflecting on the question "How would I live today, if I knew I was going to die tomorrow?"). Spend at least five to ten minutes in prayer in this way. Use the space below to journal about the experience and any changes or actions God is calling you to make in your life.

Going Deeper

THERE IS A phenomenal Lenten devotional called *Remember Your Death* by Sr. Theresa Aletheia Noble. If you feel called to use *memento mori* in a deeper way, I encourage you to pick up a copy and read it.

Day 32

Praying for Humility

HUMILITY IS CRUCIAL to our lives as followers of Christ. Just as pride is the root of all sin, humility is the foundation of all virtue. St. Francis de Sales wrote that humility was the virtue that Jesus, Mary, and all the saints cherished the most.[39] Dietrich von Hildebrand, the great philosopher and moral theologian, wrote that it is the "mother" and "fountainhead" of all other human virtues.[40] However, humility is also unfortunately one of the most misunderstood virtues.

Humility is not seeing ourselves as bad or looking down on ourselves; rather it is recognizing that everything good in us ultimately finds its source from our Creator. It is a type of intimate self-knowledge in which we are able to see how spiritually poor we would be without divine assistance. Humility is also an imitation of Jesus,

> who, though he was in the form of God, did not count equality with God a thing to be grasped, but emptied himself, taking the form of a servant, being born in the likeness of men. And being found in human form he humbled himself and became obedient unto death, even death on a cross. (Phil. 2:6–8, RSVCE)

39 St. Francis de Sales, *Philothea or An Introduction to the Devout Life* (Charlotte, NC: TAN Books, 2010).

40 Dietrich von Hildebrand, *Humility, Wellspring of Virtue* ([1948] Manchester, NH: Sophia Institute Press, 1997).

Humility not only helps us see ourselves in the right light, it helps us to see others truly as they are as sons and daughters of God. It allows us to see Christ in the poor and the marginalized, and therefore leads to other virtues such as selflessness and justice.

Scripture is filled with examples of the importance of humility, of the proud being humbled and the lowly being exalted. Jesus announced at the Sermon on the Mount, Blessed are the meek and poor! He also set an example of humility by showing how we are to serve one another when He washed the feet of His apostles (see Matt. 5:3–12 and John 13:1–17). Moreover, Jesus explained the importance of humility to His disciples in one parable on the kingdom of Heaven in which Jesus likened heaven to a wedding feast. Jesus instructed His followers that if they tried on their own to take a place of honor, they would simply bear the embarrassment of being moved lower! Instead they should take the lowest place at the feast so that they could let themselves be exalted by the master (see Luke 14:7–11).

From all of these things, it is clear that humility is important, but how exactly are we supposed to grow in it? A good place to start is simply asking for it. We need to beg God for humility so that we can grow in all the virtues and advance in our own personal journey to sainthood. Tradition has even provided us with a Litany of Humility to help us embrace this amazing and necessary virtue. A litany is a prayer composed of several different petitions, usually recited in a large group but also appropriate for private prayer. Litanies are repetitive in order to help us enter into a rhythm and reflect on the subject they encompass. The Litany of Humility is not a part of the Church's public liturgical rites, but like many other private devotionals, it is still a wonderful prayer worth exploring.

The litany itself has an unknown author. The earliest version of the prayer that we have on record comes from a book called *The Fervent Adorer* from 1867, attributed to "A Roman Catholic Clergyman."

The most popular form of the prayer was compiled by Cardinal Rafael Merry del Val y Zulueta, the secretary of state for the Vatican under Pope St. Pius X.[41]

This litany is one of the hardest prayers to pray, but it can be incredibly transformational for the interior life and the cultivation of virtue. I encourage you to pray it with an open heart, inviting the Holy Spirit to transform and enlighten you.

41 Trevor Jin, "The Litany of Humility: What Is It and Where Did It Come From?," We Dare to Say, June 26, 2021, https://wedaretosay.com/the-litany-of-humility-what-is-it-and-where-did-it-come-from/.

Action Step

FOR TODAY'S ACTION Step, we'll be praying the Litany of Humility. As you pray, consider: What line stands out to you today? Does anything you say touch on something within you that perhaps needs to be healed or confronted? Is the Holy Spirit bringing a phrase to your heart for a particular reason? Allow whatever stands out to you to become a moment of encounter between you and the Holy Spirit. Ask questions and sit silently while you ponder and pray. Like all other forms of vocal prayer, the Litany of Humility should lead to meditation and contemplation.

Begin with the Sign of the Cross.

O Jesus, meek and humble of heart,	**Hear me.**
From the desire of being esteemed,	**Deliver me, Jesus.**
From the desire of being loved,	**Deliver me, Jesus.**
From the desire of being extolled,	**Deliver me, Jesus.**
From the desire of being honored,	**Deliver me, Jesus.**
From the desire of being praised,	**Deliver me, Jesus.**
From the desire of being preferred to others,	**Deliver me, Jesus.**
From the desire of being consulted,	**Deliver me, Jesus.**
From the desire of being approved,	**Deliver me, Jesus.**
From the fear of being humiliated,	**Deliver me, Jesus.**
From the fear of being despised,	**Deliver me, Jesus.**
From the fear of suffering rebukes,	**Deliver me, Jesus.**
From the fear of being calumniated,	**Deliver me, Jesus.**
From the fear of being forgotten,	**Deliver me, Jesus.**
From the fear of being ridiculed,	**Deliver me, Jesus.**
From the fear of being wronged,	**Deliver me, Jesus.**
From the fear of being suspected,	**Deliver me, Jesus.**

That others may be loved more than I,
Jesus, grant me the grace to desire it.
That others may be esteemed more than I,
Jesus, grant me the grace to desire it.
That, in the opinion of the world,
others may increase and I may decrease,
Jesus, grant me the grace to desire it.
That others may be chosen and I set aside,
Jesus, grant me the grace to desire it.
That others may be praised and I unnoticed,
Jesus, grant me the grace to desire it.
That others may be preferred to me in everything,
Jesus, grant me the grace to desire it.
That others may become holier than I,
provided that I may become as holy as I should,
Jesus, grant me the grace to desire it.
Amen.

Chances are that this prayer was challenging or thought-provoking for you. If a word or phrase stood out to you, write it below and take it back into prayer throughout the week.

____

____

____

____

Going Deeper

IF YOU WANT to focus more on the virtue of humility in your prayer life, check out a little book called *Humility: Wellspring of Virtue* by Dietrich von Hildebrand, one of the greatest Catholic philosophers of the twentieth century.

Day 33

Spiritual Combat

WHEN PEOPLE HEAR the phrase "spiritual combat," the first thing they probably think of is exorcisms, Hollywood movies involving demons and demonic possession, or perhaps stories about the saints like Padre Pio, St. Teresa of Ávila, or St. Faustina confronting apparitions of evil spirits. If you saw the name of this chapter and were expecting (or even hoping for) stories like this, I'm sorry to say this will be far less dramatic. Though there is certainly a time and place for the ministry of exorcism, and there are many true stories about saints and Christians encountering evil spirits and casting them out, the purpose of this brief chapter is to simply shed some light on what spiritual combat looks like in the daily prayer life of someone who follows Christ.

It begins with the simple recognition that there is a spiritual reality beyond our physical one. Just as there are good spirits, called angels, there are also evil spirits, which we call demons. They are far less exciting than Hollywood makes them out to be, and they've been using the same strategies and tricks for thousands of years, but unfortunately they are quite successful a lot of the time. We've all heard at one point or another that God has a plan for our life — but we also need to recognize that the devil has his own plans to *derail* our lives. He and his demons want nothing more than for us to be miserable and cut off from divine life.

Evil spirits usually operate first by trying to stop us from praying. Second, they try to get us to give in to our vices or open ourselves up to their influence and lead us into sin. Finally, they try to trap us in a cycle of sin. Evil spirits may also feed us lies about God or make us feel shame to keep us from repenting or running back into the arms of our merciful and loving Father. The devil used these same tactics in the Garden of Eden to tempt our first parents, and he continues to utilize them today to try and lead us away from God.

Spiritual warfare first begins with examining our own hearts and praying for God's truth to shine in them. Consider your own life and think, *What are the lies that have taken root in my heart? What areas of my life have I surrendered over to sin? What vices have become strongholds for the evil one in my soul? How have I listened to the lies of the enemy and let him turn me away from prayer? How can I use my prayer time to allow God to free me from the influence of the evil one so that I can experience the true freedom of living as a co-heir of the kingdom alongside Jesus Christ?*

One of the most common ways to pray against the evil one is through prayers of renunciation. For example, if you struggle with self-worth, you might say something like, "In the name of Jesus, I renounce the lie that I'm not good enough and I accept the truth that God loves me unconditionally." Other examples of common lies are

- ✠ God doesn't love me.
- ✠ God isn't trustworthy.
- ✠ God doesn't have my best interest in mind.
- ✠ God has abandoned me.
- ✠ I am helpless or alone.
- ✠ My life has no meaning.

Sometimes the enemy may also have fed us lies about others. The devil tries to destroy relationships, especially between spouses and families. Do you sense any lies about the relationships in your life?

In addition to renouncing lies, we can also renounce the influence of evil spirits in our lives. When we give in to repeated sin, we give evil spirits a stronghold in our soul. Our will becomes weakened, and we become enslaved by the sin and quickly lose hope that we can ever break free. The truth is that Jesus wants us to be free, and repeated renunciation can be a strong prayer tool for this spiritual combat. For example, if you struggle with a fiery temper you could say, "In the name of Jesus, I renounce the spirit of anger, and I ask for the Holy Spirit to come and fill me with his peace and patience." We can also renounce the spirits of things like lust, control, selfishness, slothfulness, and addiction.

It is also worth noting that Jesus tells us in Scripture that some evil spirits only come out through prayer and fasting (see Matt. 17:21). If there is a certain sin that you are struggling with habitually and can't seem to break free, it may be time to incorporate some fasting into your spiritual battle as well. Remember the words of St. Paul: "In your struggle against sin you have not yet resisted to the point of shedding your blood" (Heb. 12:4, RSVCE).

In addition to praying against the influence of the evil one in our own lives, we can also pray against the influence of the evil one in the world and in the lives of others. For example, we can pray a Rosary for a loved one who is dabbling in New Age spirituality or witchcraft, or simply ask Jesus to be present and thwart whatever plans the evil one is trying to implement. In a sense, every time we pray an Our Father, we enter into spiritual warfare when we say, "Deliver us from evil." A common tactic of the evil one is to sow disunity and cause rifts in relationships and families through his lies and temptations.

We should also pray for the ability to recognize these tactics in order to pray against them and avoid falling into them.

As a final note, Tradition also gives us a beautiful prayer called the St. Michael Prayer that we can pray against the influence of the evil one. St. Michael is one of the archangels named in Scripture, the one who cast Satan out of heaven (see Rev. 12:7–10). His name means, "Who is like God?" which is a reminder of how humility vanquishes the evil one. You can find the words to the St. Michael Prayer in Appendix A. It is worth committing this prayer to memory and praying it in times of temptation and as an intercessory prayer for those who need deliverance.

Scripture teaches us, "For freedom Christ has set us free" (Gal. 5:1, RSVCE). When we turn to God in prayer, reject the lies of the enemy, and seek to grow in our faith, we open ourselves to experiencing the radical freedom of Christ, and we begin to grow in a desire to help others experience it as well.

✎ Action Step ✎

FOR YOUR ACTION step today, I'd like you to practice the renunciation prayer process above.

Take a few moments in prayer and ask God to reveal to you any areas in your life where the devil is actively working against you. Perhaps it is a lie that you have started to believe about yourself, or a habitual sin that you feel trapped in. What I'd like you to do is take a few moments to *renounce* those lies or spirits and *accept* the love of God and the truth that He wants to proclaim to you.

Keep in mind that the lists above are not exhaustive; it's very possible that the Holy Spirit will reveal other lies or vices that have taken root in your heart. Renounce them and proclaim the truth that burns the lie away. God wants you to be free, and He wants you to be holy. Step up to the battleground of your soul, renounce evil, and allow God's light to purify your innermost being. Fight the good fight! Go to battle against the influence of the evil one in your life and become the saint you are called to be. Use the reflection questions and journaling space below to help you with your meditation.

✠ What are the lies that the evil one tries to get you to believe?

____

____

✠ What are the truths that God wants you to speak to your heart in response to those lies?

____

____

✠ What other spirits do you renounce in the name of Jesus?

____

____

Spend some time asking God to pour His love and Spirit out on you and fill you with His peace.

Going Deeper

ONE OF THE best books about deliverance from evil spirits is a book called *Unbound: A Practical Guide to Deliverance* by Neil Lozano. In addition to the principles laid out in today's reflection, Lozano highlights several other keys for experiencing the freedom that God wants for us. *The Spiritual Combat* by Dom Lorenzo Scupoli is also an excellent book for growing in holiness. Finally, *The Screwtape Letters* by C. S. Lewis is a series of fictional letters written by a senior demon to an inferior one explaining how to go about tempting their human targets. It serves as a haunting but eye-opening glance into the reality of evil and how it seeks to lead mankind astray.

Day 34

Praying a Novena

A NOVENA IS a prayer spread out over the course of nine days, typically with some intention or petition in mind that we are bringing before God and asking Him to answer. The nine-day structure comes from the nine days between the Ascension of Jesus into heaven and the descent of the Holy Spirit at Pentecost, which the apostles spent in prayer as they waited for the Holy Spirit to fall upon them (see Acts 2). Though nine is the traditional number of days for this prayer, and where we get the word "novena" from (the Latin word for "nine" is *novem*), there are several other variations of novenas.

One of the most popular is the Novena to the Holy Spirit, which is traditionally prayed on the days from Ascension to Pentecost. There are also many novenas to saints asking them to pray for us. In recent years, the novena to Divine Mercy, a ten-day novena that is prayed from Good Friday to Divine Mercy Sunday, has grown in popularity. Basically, any prayer can become a novena. It takes discipline and the proper mindset to remember to pray the same prayer, usually for the same intention, every day, but praying novenas is a beautiful way to strengthen your prayer life and your relationship with God.

However, we should always keep in mind that novenas are not magical recipes of prayer to get what we want. God is God and we are not God, and His answer to our prayers is sometimes different from what we want. Yes, miracles can and do happen, but not always, and not always in the ways that we hope for or expect. We cannot manipulate God, and we should never try to reduce our prayer to a superstitious formula that will automatically get us what we want like some sort of get-out-of-suffering-free card. Our disposition should always be, "Lord, please answer this prayer intention in the way that I am asking you to, but ultimately I know you have a plan, so let your will be done, and help me to be at peace with whatever happens." We don't pray a novena for nine days because there is magic power in the number nine; we pray for nine days (or sometimes more) because it helps us to unite our prayers with those of the Church through her Tradition, and it helps us to remember the saving power of the Holy Spirit, bringing to mind those nine days of prayer before Pentecost.

But there is one prayer intention that God always answers: "Lord, give me more of your Holy Spirit." In Luke 18:1–8, Jesus speaks of the importance of persistence in prayer. We should continue to bring our petitions before God daily, but the ultimate gift — the thing that God always gives us in prayer even when we don't get what we originally wanted — is Himself. Come Holy Spirit!

✎ Action Step ✎

FOR OUR ACTION step today, we'll be praying Mother Teresa's "flying novena." I heard about this prayer several years ago, and it has become my go-to in many situations. At its heart, it is a call to Mary, the Blessed Mother, for help, asking her to pray for us and whatever intentions we have. It's a great prayer for whenever you hear of a tragic event or when someone asks for prayers, but I also use it before setting out to accomplish a big task and before speaking and music engagements. The flying novena has become for me an incredible source of peace in times when I've felt anxious or stressed.

What sets Mother Teresa's flying novena apart from a traditional novena is the fact that it can be done in just a few minutes rather than over nine or more days. It is incredibly simple: it consists of praying the *Memorare,* an ancient prayer invoking the Blessed Mother for help, ten times in a row. Here are the words to the prayer:

> Remember, O most gracious Virgin Mary, that never was it known that anyone who fled to your protection, implored your help, or sought your intercession was left unaided. Inspired with this confidence, I fly unto you, O Virgin of virgins, my Mother. To you I come, before you I stand, sinful and sorrowful. O Mother of the Word incarnate, despise not my petitions, but in your clemency hear and answer me. Amen.

Why do we pray *ten* Memorares instead of nine, the typical number that is associated with novenas? The answer is simple: the tenth is offered as a prayer of thanksgiving in anticipation of God answering the request. In other words, it is a prayer of entrusting ourselves to whatever God has in store for us, and knowing that we can rest in the mantle of the Blessed Mother, no matter what comes our way![42]

Going Deeper

You can find dozens of novenas at www.praymorenovenas.com. I encourage you to check out this website and consider scheduling a novena around a certain feast day or intention that you'd like to pray for. Feel free to use the space below to write out certain feast days, saints, or petitions that you would like to build a novena around.

____

____

____

____

____

____

[42] Joseph Pronechen, "How to Pray Mother Teresa's Famous Emergency 'Flying Novena' to Our Lady," National Catholic Register, September 5, 2019, https://www.ncregister.com/blog/how-to-pray-mother-teresa-s-famous-flying-novena-to-our-lady.

Day 35

Being Embraced by Divine Mercy

ON FEBRUARY 22, 1931, Jesus appeared to a young nun in Poland named Faustina Kowalska for the first time, bringing her a message of Divine Mercy that He wished to share with the whole world. Under obedience to her religious superiors, St. Faustina recorded her conversations with Jesus. The message itself is quite simple—as one particularly devoted religious order puts it, as simple as ABC.[43]

A — Ask for God's mercy

B — Be merciful toward others

C — Completely trust in Jesus

According to the Marian Fathers, there are five main elements to keeping the Divine Mercy devotion: celebrating the feast day, venerating the Divine Mercy image, praying the Divine Mercy novena, praying during the hour of Divine Mercy, and praying the Divine Mercy chaplet. For our purposes, we'll be focusing primarily on the chaplet, but I recommend learning more about this beautiful devotion by visiting

[43] "The Divine Mercy Message and Devotion," Marian Fathers of the Immaculate Conception, accessed November 27, 2024, https://www.thedivinemercy.org/message.

www.thedivinemercy.org or checking out some of the other resources in the Going Deeper section.

The intention and wording of the Divine Mercy chaplet is simple. It is ultimately a prayer asking for God to pour out His Divine Mercy on souls, especially those who need it the most. The prayers of the chaplet are said on rosary beads, but if you don't have a rosary to count ten beads on, your fingers will work in a pinch as well. Here are the prayers that are said.

1. **Make the sign of the Cross**

   In the name of the Father, and of the Son, and of the Holy Spirit. Amen.

2. **Optional opening prayers (St. Faustina's Prayer for Sinners)**

   O Jesus, eternal Truth, our Life, I call upon You and I beg Your mercy for poor sinners. O sweetest Heart of my Lord, full of pity and unfathomable mercy, I plead with You for poor sinners. O Most Sacred Heart, Fount of Mercy from which gush forth rays of inconceivable graces upon the entire human race, I beg of You light for poor sinners. O Jesus, be mindful of Your own bitter Passion and do not permit the loss of souls redeemed at so dear a price of Your most precious Blood. O Jesus, when I consider the great price of Your Blood, I rejoice at its immensity, for one drop alone would have been enough for the salvation of all sinners. Although sin is an abyss of wickedness and ingratitude, the price paid for us can never be equaled. Therefore, let every soul trust in the Passion of the Lord, and place its hope in His mercy. God will not deny His mercy to anyone. Heaven and earth may change, but God's mercy will never be exhausted. Oh, what immense joy burns in my heart when I contemplate Your incomprehensible goodness, O Jesus! I desire to bring all sinners to Your feet that they may glorify Your mercy throughout endless ages.[44]

You expired, Jesus, but the source of life gushed forth for souls, and the ocean of mercy opened up for the whole world. O Fount of Life, unfathomable Divine Mercy, envelop the whole world and empty Yourself out upon us. O Blood and Water, which gushed forth from the Heart of Jesus as a fount of mercy for us, I trust in You! [Repeat this last line three times.]

3. Our Father

Our Father, Who art in heaven, hallowed be Thy name; Thy kingdom come; Thy will be done on earth as it is in heaven. Give us this day our daily bread; and forgive us our trespasses as we forgive those who trespass against us; and lead us not into temptation, but deliver us from evil, Amen.

4. Hail Mary

Hail Mary, full of grace. The Lord is with thee. Blessed art thou among women, and blessed is the fruit of thy womb, Jesus. Holy Mary, Mother of God, pray for us sinners, now and at the hour of our death, Amen.

5. The Apostles' Creed

I believe in God, the Father almighty, Creator of heaven and earth, and in Jesus Christ, His only Son, our Lord, who was conceived by the Holy Spirit, born of the Virgin Mary,

[44] *The Diary of Saint Maria Faustina Kowalska*, p. 37, entry 72.

suffered under Pontius Pilate, was crucified, died and was buried; He descended into hell; on the third day He rose again from the dead; He ascended into heaven, and is seated at the right hand of God the Father almighty; from there He will come to judge the living and the dead. I believe in the Holy Spirit, the holy catholic Church, the communion of saints, the forgiveness of sins, the resurrection of the body, and life everlasting. Amen.

6. The Eternal Father

Eternal Father, I offer you the Body and Blood, Soul and Divinity of Your Dearly Beloved Son, Our Lord, Jesus Christ, in atonement for our sins and those of the whole world.

7. On the 10 small beads of each decade

For the sake of His sorrowful Passion, have mercy on us and on the whole world.

8. Repeat for the remaining decades

Say the "Eternal Father" (6) on the "Our Father" bead.

Say ten "For the sake of His sorrowful Passion" (7) on the "Hail Mary" beads. [Do this for all five decades.]

9. Conclude with Holy God [Repeat three times]

Holy God, Holy Mighty One, Holy Immortal One, have mercy on us and on the whole world.

10. Optional closing prayers

Eternal God, in whom mercy is endless and the treasury of compassion inexhaustible, look kindly upon us and increase Your mercy in us, that in difficult moments we might not despair nor become despondent, but with great confidence submit ourselves to Your holy will, which is Love and Mercy itself.

O Greatly Merciful God, Infinite Goodness, today all mankind calls out from the abyss of its misery to Your mercy — to Your compassion, O God; and it is with its mighty voice of misery that it cries out. Gracious God, do not reject the prayer of this earth's exiles! O Lord, Goodness beyond our understanding, Who are acquainted with our misery through and through, and know that by our own power we cannot ascend to You, we implore You: anticipate us with Your grace and keep on increasing Your mercy in us, that we may faithfully do Your holy will all through our life and at death's hour. Let the omnipotence of Your mercy shield us from the darts of our salvation's enemies, that we may with confidence, as Your children, await Your [Son's] final coming — that day known to You alone. And we expect to obtain everything promised us by Jesus in spite of all our wretchedness. For Jesus is our Hope: through His merciful Heart, as through an open gate, we pass through to heaven.[45]

[45] *The Diary of Saint Maria Faustina Kowalska*, p. 557, entry 1570.

Action Step

USING THE INSTRUCTIONS above, pray a chaplet of Divine Mercy. This prayer does not take long, but it is incredibly powerful. If you have a set of rosary beads, use them to help you engage your mind and body and enter more deeply into prayer. As you pray, ask God to open your heart to His love and mercy. Put yourself in God's presence and allow Him to embrace you.

After you pray, use the space below to write about this prayer experience. How did this type of prayer make you feel? Did anything stand out to you during your prayer time? Do any questions or thoughts come to the surface of your mind? Allow this space to be a dialogue between you and God.

____

____

____

____

Going Deeper

TO LEARN MORE about the Divine Mercy devotion, I recommend checking out thedivinemercy.org. There are also many wonderful books out there, such as *7 Secrets of Divine Mercy* by Vinny Flynn and *The Second Greatest Story Ever Told* by Fr. Michael Gaitley, M.I.C. Of course, *The Diary of St. Faustina* is also a wonderful insight into St. Faustina's intimacy with Jesus, and reveals the depths of His merciful love in a powerful way.

Day 36

Praying with the Saints

Today we're going to tackle one of the more controversial topics in modern Christian history — the saints! Unfortunately, there is a lot of confusion about what Catholics really believe about the saints, especially for those from other Christian denominations. To be honest, it's not hard to understand their confusion. Imagine walking into a Catholic church for the first time with no knowledge of Catholic traditions or teachings and seeing all the statues of historical figures with dozens of candles burning in front of them. Your very first thought might be, *Why do Catholics worship all these people?*

The reality is that Catholics don't worship the saints. Worship is reserved for God alone. We revere the saints, we look to them as models of holiness, and we ask them to pray and intercede for us. In a sense, we see the Church as one big family — and the saints are our big brothers and big sisters! We celebrate their lives and the way that they gave glory to God with their lives, and we ask them to pray for us because they are part of our Church and part of the family of God.

The follow-up question that people often have is then, "Why?" Why do we ask the saints for intercession instead of going directly to Jesus? Doesn't the Bible say that there is only one mediator between God and man, and that the mediator is Jesus (see 1 Tim. 2:5)? Why bother adding another layer or middleman?

To this I would respond, well, of course we should go directly to Jesus, and we should do it often! A personal relationship with Jesus Christ is the foundation of the Christian journey, and it is the call of every disciple to grow in this relationship and put it above all else. But God, in His loving goodness, created a world where our relationships with others matter. Each of us plays a role in the spiritual life of others, and we are each called to lead people closer to God. This mission, and the joy that comes with it, continues after we die.

Everyone who is in heaven is considered a saint, but in many cases people live such a model life of holiness that they become formally recognized and canonized by the Church. Having said that, even among canonized saints there are certain standouts who seem to have a reputation for being more visibly active than others in the world! Sometimes, certain saints seem to pop into our lives frequently — we start to see their name everywhere, they get brought up in conversations with people, or we simply start to feel drawn to a certain person (some of my friends and I affectionately call this "holy stalking"). When this happens, it may be a sign that this saint wants to be a more active part of your spiritual journey. Some particular saints may even be reaching out to us in certain periods of life to help us out, especially if they went through similar experiences in their own earthly life.

Having a devotion to and praying to a particular saint should never be reduced to a superstitious formula of simply saying a prayer out loud. It should be relational. We should seek to learn more about the saint and to talk to them as we would a friend, because they *are* our friends. When we grow close to certain saints, it is like growing in a friendship with someone who lives a great distance away — almost like a pen pal of sorts.

Finally, I like to think of praying with and through the saints as a sort of magnifying glass for our prayer. Just as light becomes focused and more intense when it passes through a magnifying glass, the saints help refine our prayer. There is a true spiritual power in intercession—praying for other people. The saints are the greatest intercessors around! You can think of them as professional pray-ers who take your intentions and needs and pray to God on your behalf for you. When you get to know them and make them present in your life, their prayers for you will help your spiritual life grow and flourish.

Action Step

FOR TODAY'S ACTION step, we'll be praying the Litany of Saints, an ancient prayer of the Church that traces its roots back to the fifth century. It is one of six litanies approved for use in the liturgy by the Church and is prayed at the Easter Vigil Mass and on the Feast of All Saints (November 1). The Litany of Saints is also often included in funeral rites and the rite of Baptism. In many of these celebrations, the litany is sung or chanted rather than recited.[46]

The Litany of the Saints is most commonly prayed in liturgical prayer, but it can be prayed on your own as well. When prayed in a group, one person prays the first part of each line, and the rest of the group prays the response, which has been set in bold to make things easier. As always, pray it slowly and carefully. As you pray it, I encourage you to see if any of these saints' names stand out to you. Take some time later on to learn about them.

The prayer itself is structured into several different movements. Like many other litanies and liturgical prayers, it begins by calling upon God to show His mercy to us. From there, we go to the various saints of the litany, asking them to pray for us, before we turn our focus back to God, spiritually accompanied now by the heavenly hosts of saints in our prayer. We end once more by invoking God's mercy in a spirit of humble thanksgiving.

As you pray, try to write down or highlight any names and phrases that pop out at you. If there is a word or phrase you don't understand, write it down and look it up later. Enter into this prayer

[46] "The Litany of the Saints," Our Catholic Prayers, accessed November 27, 2024, https://www.ourcatholicprayers.com/litany-of-the-saints.html.

with an open heart, and ask the Holy Spirit to quiet your mind and your soul as you begin.

Lord, have mercy on us. **Lord, have mercy on us.**
Christ, have mercy on us. **Christ, have mercy on us.**
Lord, have mercy on us. **Lord, have mercy on us.**
Christ, hear us. **Christ, graciously hear us.**
God, the Father of Heaven, **have mercy on us.**
God the Son, Redeemer of the world, **have mercy on us.**
God the Holy Spirit, **have mercy on us.**
Holy Trinity, one God, **have mercy on us.**

Holy Mary, **pray for us.**
Holy Mother of God, **pray for us.**
Holy Virgin of Virgins, **pray for us.**
St. Michael, **pray for us.**
St. Gabriel, **pray for us.**
St. Raphael, **pray for us.**
All you Holy Angels and Archangels **pray for us.**
St. John the Baptist, **pray for us.**
St. Joseph, **pray for us.**
All you Holy Patriarchs and Prophets, **pray for us.**
St. Peter, **pray for us.**
St. Paul, **pray for us.**
St. Andrew, **pray for us.**
St. James, **pray for us.**
St. John, **pray for us.**
St. Thomas, **pray for us.**
St. James, **pray for us.**
St. Philip, **pray for us.**
St. Bartholomew, **pray for us.**
St. Matthew, **pray for us.**
St. Simon, **pray for us.**
St. Jude, **pray for us.**
St. Matthias, **pray for us.**
St. Barnabas, **pray for us.**

St. Luke,	**pray for us.**
St. Mark,	**pray for us.**
All you Holy Apostles and Evangelists,	**pray for us.**
All you Holy Disciples of the Lord,	**pray for us.**
All you Holy Innocents,	**pray for us.**
St. Stephen,	**pray for us.**
St. Lawrence,	**pray for us.**
St. Vincent,	**pray for us.**
St. Fabian and Sebastian,	**pray for us.**
St. John and Paul,	**pray for us.**
St. Cosmas and Damian,	**pray for us.**
All you Holy Martyrs,	**pray for us.**
St. Sylvester,	**pray for us.**
St. Gregory,	**pray for us.**
St. Ambrose,	**pray for us.**
St. Augustine,	**pray for us.**
St. Jerome,	**pray for us.**
St. Martin,	**pray for us.**
St. Nicholas,	**pray for us.**
All you Holy Bishops and Confessors,	**pray for us.**
All you Holy Doctors,	**pray for us.**
St. Anthony,	**pray for us.**
St. Benedict,	**pray for us.**
St. Bernard,	**pray for us.**
St. Dominic,	**pray for us.**
St. Francis,	**pray for us.**
All you Holy Priests and Levites,	**pray for us.**
All you Holy Monks and Hermits,	**pray for us.**
St. Mary Magdalene,	**pray for us.**
St. Agatha,	**pray for us.**
St. Lucy,	**pray for us.**
St. Agnes,	**pray for us.**
St. Cecilia,	**pray for us.**
St. Anastasia,	**pray for us.**
St. Catherine,	**pray for us.**
St. Clare,	**pray for us.**

All you Holy Virgins and Widows, **pray for us.**
All you Holy Saints of God, **pray for us.**

Lord, be merciful, **Lord, save your people.**
From all evil, **Lord, save your people.**
From all sin, **Lord, save your people.**
From your wrath, **Lord, save your people.**
From a sudden and unprovided death, **Lord, save your people.**
From the snares of the devil, **Lord, save your people.**
From anger, hatred, and all ill-will, **Lord, save your people.**
From the spirit of uncleanness, **Lord, save your people.**
From lightning and tempest, **Lord, save your people.**
From the scourge of earthquake, **Lord, save your people.**
From plague, famine, and war, **Lord, save your people.**
From everlasting death, **Lord, save your people.**

By the mystery of your Holy Incarnation, **Lord, save your people.**
By Your Coming, **Lord, save your people.**
By Your Birth, **Lord, save your people.**
By Your Baptism and Holy Fasting, **Lord, save your people.**
By Your Cross and Passion, **Lord, save your people.**
By Your Death and Burial, **Lord, save your people.**
By Your Holy Resurrection, **Lord, save your people.**
By Your wonderful Ascension, **Lord, save your people.**
By the coming of the Holy Spirit, **Lord, save your people.**
On the Day of Judgment, **Lord, save your people.**

Be merciful to us sinners, **Lord, hear our prayer.**
That you will spare us, **Lord, hear our prayer.**
That you will pardon us, **Lord, hear our prayer.**
That it may please you to bring us to true penance, **Lord, hear our prayer.**
Guide and protect your holy Church, **Lord, hear our prayer.**
Preserve in holy religion the Pope, and all those in holy orders, **Lord, hear our prayer.**

Lord, hear our prayer.

Humble the enemies of holy Church,	**Lord, hear our prayer.**
Give peace and unity to the whole Christian people,	**Lord, hear our prayer.**
Bring back to the unity of the Church all those who are straying, and bring all unbelievers to the light of the gospel,	**Lord, hear our prayer.**
Strengthen and preserve us in your holy service,	**Lord, hear our prayer.**
Raise our minds to desire the things of heaven,	**Lord, hear our prayer.**
Reward all our benefactors with eternal blessings,	**Lord, hear our prayer.**
Deliver our souls from eternal damnation, and the souls of our brethren, relatives, and benefactors,	**Lord, hear our prayer.**
Give and preserve the fruits of the earth,	**Lord, hear our prayer.**
Grant eternal rest to all the faithful departed,	**Lord, hear our prayer.**
That it may please You to hear and heed us, Jesus, Son of the Living God,	**Lord, hear our prayer.**
Lamb of God, who takes away the sins of the world,	**Spare us, O Lord!**
Lamb of God, who takes away the sins of the world,	**Graciously hear us, O Lord!**
Lamb of God, who takes away the sins of the world,	**Have mercy on us.**
Christ, hear us,	**Christ, graciously hear us**
Lord Jesus, hear our prayer	**Lord Jesus, hear our prayer.**
Lord, have mercy on us	**Lord, have mercy on us.**

Christ, have mercy on us	**Christ, have mercy on us.**
Lord, have mercy on us	**Lord, have mercy on us.**
Amen.	

Going Deeper

THERE ARE MANY wonderful books about the lives of the saints, far too many to list here. Your best bet is to start by picking a saint whom you'd like to learn more about, and then find some good books about their life. Over the course of the next couple of days, we'll be learning about the greatest of the saints, the Blessed Mother!

PART 11

Marian Prayer

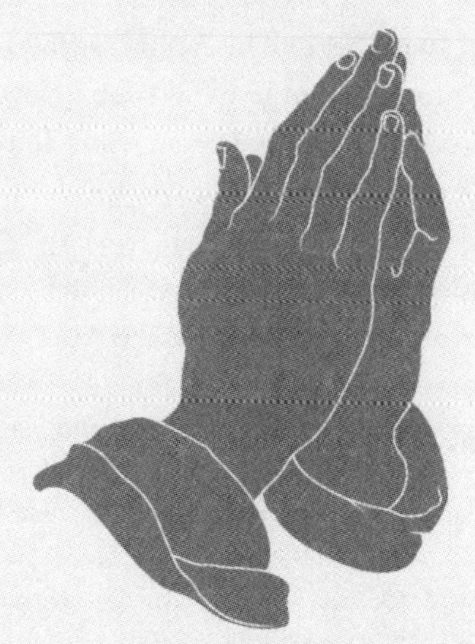

In the Church's history, no saint is more revered than the Blessed Mother. She is the first and greatest of all of the saints, because she was and is the person closest to Jesus. Jesus came to the world through Mary, and it is through Mary that countless souls are drawn closer to Jesus.

Unfortunately, just as we saw in yesterday's reflection with the saints, there is often confusion about Mary's role in the Church. A lot of people believe that Catholics *worship* Mary, and that simply isn't true. We revere her as Jesus' mother, we venerate her role in salvation history, and we believe that she is our spiritual mother. Mary's "yes" to God was the catalyst for Jesus' redeeming sacrifice, and Mary was an active participant at every key moment in Jesus' earthly ministry, especially during His Passion. Moreover, before giving His life on the Cross, Jesus gave His mother to the Church, as represented by the beloved disciple taking her into his home (see John 19:25–27). Each of us is called to cooperate in Jesus' mission to save souls, but Mary played a key role in this work while on earth, and she continues to play a crucial part in evangelizing and praying for the world today.

The Church holds four dogmas about Mary. These are doctrinal statements that state clearly what the Church teaches about our Blessed Mother and are considered essential to Catholic belief:

1. *Mary is the Mother of God.* This is quite simple — Jesus is God, and Mary is the mother of Jesus, so Mary is the mother of God! In the ancient Israelite kingdom, the mother of the king had a special role in helping to govern the kingdom, and we find the same thing in the new kingdom as well.

2. *Mary was immaculately conceived.* This means that she was free from original sin at the moment of conception in order to prepare her for her unique role in conceiving Jesus by the power of the Holy Spirit. When the archangel Gabriel greets Mary, he exclaims that she is "full of grace." This key phrase means that Mary had already been filled with saving grace in a mysterious way by the power of God, even though Jesus had not yet completed His saving work of redemption at that time. Mary is still saved by Jesus, but His graces were applied to her ahead of time.

3. *Mary was a perpetual virgin.* Jesus had no earthly father. When she received the news that she was to bear a son, Mary asked how this was to be, for she had "no relations with a man" (Luke 1:34, NABRE), even though she was about to get married. In looking at this response and understanding Jewish culture in the first century, it's likely that Mary had taken a vow of chastity, of which St. Joseph would have been well aware. Sometimes, people argue that the Gospels say that Jesus had siblings (see Matt. 12:46–50), but there are two easy explanations that could account for this verbiage. The word for "sibling" used here in the Greek translates more exactly to "brethren" and was a word that could also include cousins, townmates, and anyone that would be considered kin. These siblings also could have been Joseph's children from an earlier marriage. Either way, from the earliest days of the Church, Christians have held the truth that Mary was perpetually a virgin.

4. *Mary was assumed into heaven — body and soul.* Either she was carried up directly into heaven while still alive like the prophets Elijah and Enoch from the Old Testament, or immediately after death her body was

> lifted up or disappeared into heaven, just like some early Jewish traditions claim happened to Moses.

There are many wonderful books about Mary and how to grow closer to her. Some of them are referenced in the pages ahead. Most importantly, however, is the simple truth that Mary loves us and is our caring mother. She wants nothing more than to lead us to her son, Jesus. When we entrust ourselves to Mary, we are taking the shortest of shortcuts to holiness and to Jesus. Just as He came to us through her, we can go to Him through her. As one catchy phrase puts it, "Know Mary, know Jesus. No Mary, no Jesus!"

Day 37

The Rosary

WHEN PEOPLE THINK of Marian prayer, the first thing that comes to mind is likely the Rosary. The Rosary is a beautiful prayer; incredibly simple, yet its depths are boundless. It consists of a series of vocal prayers and meditation, with some room for contemplation built in as well. It is most often prayed on a set of rosary beads, but there are other ways to pray it as well such as the rosary ring or simply keeping track of counting with your fingers.

Praying a Rosary begins with the following vocal prayers:

- ✠ One Apostles' Creed
- ✠ One Our Father for the Pope and his intentions
- ✠ Three Hail Marys for an outpouring of the virtues of faith, hope, and charity
- ✠ One Glory Be

After these introductory prayers, we pray through a set of decades. The vocal prayer of each decade consists of one Our Father, ten Hail Marys, one Glory Be, and often one Fatima Prayer. The meditative prayer of each decade consists of reflecting on key moments in the lives of Jesus or Mary. As we meditate on each moment, or mystery, we pray with Mary and we ask her to intercede for us.

In total there are twenty mysteries that we may reflect on in the Rosary. Each day has a different set of mysteries assigned to it. We typically choose which mysteries we are going to meditate on based on what day of the week it is. By doing this, we unite ourselves spiritually with the countless others who are praying and meditating on the same mysteries that day. Sometimes, however, people may choose to meditate upon decades that don't necessarily align with the traditional days, and that is ok! For example, some people may choose to pray the Joyful Mysteries more in Advent and Christmas, and the Sorrowful Mysteries in Lent. Usually, people will only pray one set of mysteries for a specific day, but sometimes people may pray all twenty in one sitting. The mysteries are split into four sets of five, as follows:

The Joyful Mysteries
(prayed on Mondays and Saturdays)

- ✠ The Annunciation to Mary: Luke 1:26–38
- ✠ The Visitation of Mary to Elizabeth: Luke 1:39–45
- ✠ The Nativity of Jesus: Luke 2:1–12
- ✠ The Presentation of Jesus in the Temple: Luke 2:22–38
- ✠ The Finding of the Child Jesus in the Temple: Luke 2:41–52

The Luminous Mysteries
(prayed on Thursdays)

- ✠ The Baptism of Jesus: Matthew 3:13–17
- ✠ The Wedding at Cana: John 2:1–11

- ✠ The Proclamation That the Kingdom of Heaven Is at Hand: Mark 1:14–15
- ✠ The Transfiguration of Jesus: Matthew 17:1–8
- ✠ The Institution of the Eucharist: Matthew 26:26–30

THE SORROWFUL MYSTERIES (PRAYED ON TUESDAYS AND FRIDAYS)

- ✠ Jesus' Agony in the Garden: Matthew 26:36–46
- ✠ The Scourging of Jesus: John 19:1
- ✠ The Crowning with Thorns: John 19:2–3
- ✠ Jesus Carries His Cross: Matthew 27:32
- ✠ The Crucifixion and Death of Jesus: John 19:16–30

THE GLORIOUS MYSTERIES (PRAYED ON WEDNESDAYS AND SUNDAYS)

- ✠ The Resurrection of Jesus: Matthew 28:1–10
- ✠ The Ascension of Jesus into Heaven: Acts 1:6–12
- ✠ The Coming of the Holy Spirit at Pentecost: Acts 2:1–4
- ✠ The Assumption of Mary into Heaven
- ✠ The Crowning of Mary as Queen of Heaven and Earth

Each decade is prayed by first taking time to meditate and reflect on the mystery. Then we pray the vocal prayers. We are also encouraged to take a few moments in silence at the end of the decade to simply rest in God's presence (contemplative prayer).

After all five decades are complete, we conclude with one Hail Holy Queen and the Rosary Conclusion prayer. Sometimes people may also add in the Prayer to St. Michael or a brief litany of their favorite saints as well.

Praying the Rosary is prayer with Mary, who always leads us closer to Jesus. It is a beautiful way to reflect on Jesus' and Mary's lives and grow closer to both of them.

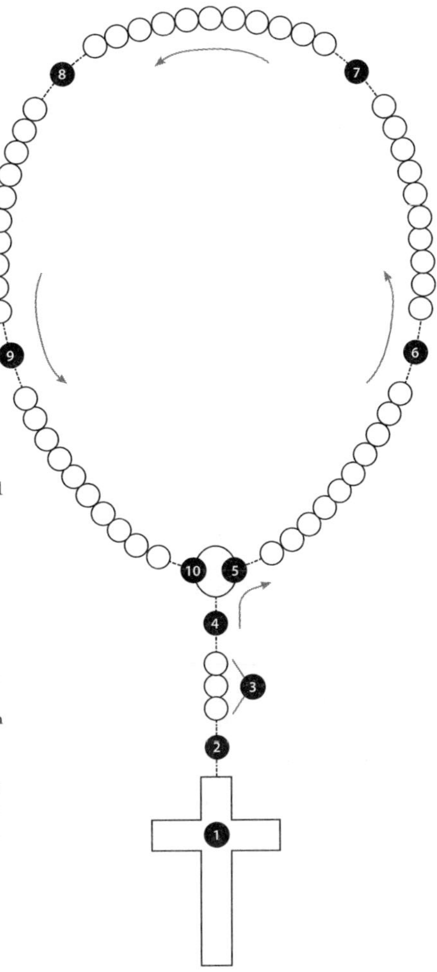

1. Sign of the Cross, prayers for the intentions of the Pope, and the Apostles' Creed
or Sign of the Cross and Psalm 70:1

2. Our Father

3. Three Hail Marys

4. Glory Be

5. Announce the first mystery, read a relevant Scripture passage, pause for a few moments of silence. Then pray the Our Father, ten Hail Marys (one for each bead, adding the suggested clause or one of your own after the name of Jesus, while meditating on the First Mystery), a Glory Be, the Fatima Prayer, and the Concluding Prayer.

6-9. Repeat the sequence for the remaining decades, meditating on the Second, Third, Fourth, and Fifth Mysteries.

10. Pray the Hail, Holy Queen, the Concluding Prayer, and the Saint Michael Prayer (optional), and the Sign of the Cross.

Action Step

PRAY THE ROSARY! All the prayers for the Rosary are found at the back of this book in Appendix A. If you don't have time to pray the full five decades, simply pick a single decade and mystery that you feel called to reflect on and pray with. Be sure to leave some time for silent contemplation at the end. Feel free to use the space below to write about your thoughts or experience with this prayer.

____

____

____

____

Going Deeper

THE BEST BOOK to learn more about the Rosary is *Champions of the Rosary* by Fr. Don Calloway, especially if you want to read about the history and practicality of this incredible prayer! *The Secret of the Rosary* by St. Louis de Montfort is another great book about this devotion.

Day 38

The Angelus and Regina Caeli

THE ANGELUS IS a beautiful prayer tradition that receives its name from the first line of the prayer "Angelus Domini nuntiavit Mariæ," or in English, "The angel of the Lord declared unto Mary." It is a reflection on the Incarnation, the most sacred moment in human history. It also is a reflection on the Annunciation and Mary's wonderful consent to becoming the Mother of Jesus! Traditionally, it is prayed three times each day, at 6 a.m., noon, and 6 p.m., as a way of sanctifying the whole day. It is believed to have grown out of an ancient tradition of reciting three Hail Marys at the ringing of the church bells at these hours.

In addition to the Hail Marys, the Angelus also contains three brief antiphons before each of them and a closing prayer at the end. When prayed in a group, the leader says the first line, marked with a ℣. (for "versicle," a short prayer calling for a response) and the rest of the group says the response marked with an ℟. The full text for the Angelus reads as follows:

℣. The Angel of the Lord declared unto Mary.
℟. And she conceived of the Holy Spirit.
Hail Mary . . .

℣. Behold the handmaid of the Lord.
℟. Be it done unto me according to your word.
Hail Mary . . .

℣. And the Word was made Flesh.
℟. And dwelt among us.
Hail Mary …

℣. Pray for us, O holy Mother of God.
℟. That we may be made worthy of the promises of Christ.

Let us pray:

Pour forth, we beseech you, O Lord, your grace into our hearts; that we, to whom the Incarnation of Christ, your Son, was made known by the message of an angel, may by His Passion and Cross be brought to the glory of His Resurrection. Through the same Christ, our Lord. Amen.

In medieval times, when the bells rang, everyone stopped what they were doing to pray this prayer together. It was built into the fabric of society, and its simplicity ensured that everyone could pray it. One of the things that I personally appreciate about this devotion is the way that it interrupts us in order to call our attention to the Lord. It reminds us to stop and take a break to draw our attention to God, even if it's just for a few moments. We don't pray the Angelus when we are done with whatever we are working on, we pray it when it is time to do so and put everything else on hold. What a wonderful message this helps us internalize: as important as work is, God is more important. Therefore, for those few minutes each day, we can put work aside and recall what He has done for us.

By keeping the Angelus devotion, we place the central truth of our Faith close to our minds and hearts. With Mary's response to the angel, human history was radically changed forever. In this prayer we recall these moments, but we also ask Mary to pray for us and beg God to send His grace upon our hearts and bring us to the glory of Jesus' Resurrection. It is a powerful prayer! It is also one that has the Church's full support and backing. Many Popes have written about the graces poured out on those who keep this devotion, and Pope Francis (along with his predecessors Pope Benedict XVI and Pope St. John Paul II) leads a public recitation of the Angelus every week on Sundays when he is in the Vatican.

Similar to the Angelus, Tradition has also given us the Regina Caeli prayer. Like the Angelus, we don't know the source of the Regina Caeli devotion, which borrows words from the ancient hymn of the same name. The Regina Caeli is prayed instead of the Angelus during the liturgical season of Easter. Whereas the Angelus gives us a Marian lens on the Annunciation, the Regina Caeli gives us a Marian lens on the Resurrection:

℣. Queen of Heaven, rejoice, alleluia.
℟. For He whom you did merit to bear, alleluia.
Hail Mary . . .

℣. Has risen, as he said, alleluia.
℟. Pray for us to God, alleluia.
Hail Mary . . .

℣. Rejoice and be glad, O Virgin Mary, alleluia.
℟. For the Lord has truly risen, alleluia.
Hail Mary . . .

Let us pray:

Let us pray. O God, who gave joy to the world through the resurrection of Thy Son, our Lord Jesus Christ, grant we beseech Thee, that through the intercession of the Virgin Mary, His Mother, we may obtain the joys of everlasting life. Through the same Christ our Lord. Amen.

✎ Action Step ✎

Your action step today is to pray the Angelus (or Regina Caeli if it is in the season of Easter) at the traditionally designated times for the next twenty-four hours. Set reminders or alarms at noon, 6 p.m., and 6 a.m. to pray this devotion. If 6 a.m. is too early for you, you can set your morning reminder for 8 a.m. or whenever you wake up. The important thing is that the reminder interrupts whatever you are doing in order to put first things first and spend a few moments in prayer.

Going Deeper

If you'd like to incorporate this devotion more deeply into your life, I encourage you to set reminders or an alarm on your phone or somewhere visible and simply start praying it every day. You don't have to pray at all three hours. Try starting with just praying this at noon each day and from there you can add the other two hours if you wish. A book called *Praying the Angelus: Find Joy, Peace, and Purpose in Everyday Life* by Jared Dees is worth checking out if you want to learn more about this prayer.

Day 39

Wearing a Scapular or Miraculous Medal

ON JULY 16, 1251, the Blessed Mother appeared to St. Simon Stock, the leader of the Carmelite order at the time, and promised him that whoever faithfully wears her scapular will not suffer the eternal fire. Of course, it is not the scapular itself or even the Blessed Mother that causes salvation; only Jesus is our savior. The scapular is therefore not worn out of any superstitious belief but simply as a way to remind us to keep an inward disposition of love and reverence toward God.

Keeping the scapular devotion consists of two primary conditions — faithfully wearing the scapular as a reminder and sign of devotion to Jesus through the Blessed Mother and trying one's best to live out the Christian Faith. Of course, we should always strive for this second objective, yet we can rest assured that if we faithfully wear the scapular and ask Mary for her prayers, she will be praying and interceding for us at all times, especially at the hour of our death.[47]

The scapular itself is simple — two pieces of brown cloth connected with string laces. Images of Mary and St. Simon Stock along with the words of her promise are often printed on the material.

[47] William Most, "The Brown Scapular," EWTN, accessed November 27, 2024, https://www.ewtn.com/catholicism/library/brown-scapular-12443.

Although the brown scapular is the original and most popular scapular devotion, there are also many other colors that each have different promises or graces attached to them. For example, the red scapular is a reminder of the blood that was shed for us by Christ, and in an apparition Jesus promised that all who wear it would receive an outpouring of deeper faith, hope, and charity every Friday that they wear it. Likewise, there is a green scapular that plays a special role in evangelization and conversion of hearts. The Church has approved over fifteen different types of scapular devotion that consist of a wide range of spiritualities.

Scapular.

The scapular isn't the only wearable holy item that was given to the world by the Blessed Mother. In 1830 Mary appeared to a young girl named Catherine Laboure. In the apparition, St. Catherine saw Mary standing upon a globe with rays of light pouring forth from her hands and the inscription "O Mary, conceived without sin, pray for us who have recourse to thee" framed around her. Mary asked St. Catherine to have a medal made with the image shown and promised incredible graces to those who wear it.

On the front side of the medal we see the image of Mary just as she appeared to St. Catherine Laboure. On the back, we see the Cross and a large M intertwined, highlighting the close relationship that Jesus and Mary had and the suffering and anguish that both felt at Calvary. Though Mary did not physically suffer, spiritually and emotionally she went through the torment of watching her son go

Miraculous Medal.

through His mission and stayed by His side the whole time. Below this sign are the images of the Sacred Heart of Jesus and the Immaculate Heart of Mary, and along the outside we see twelve stars signifying the twelve tribes of Israel, the twelve apostles, and the crown of twelve stars we see upon Mary in Revelation 12. The prayer itself recalls the doctrine of the Immaculate Conception and highlights the intercessory role that Mary plays in the lives of Christians.

Countless miracles are attributed to Mary's Miraculous Medal because our spiritual mother Mary is still interceding for us and taking our intentions to her son—just as she did at the wedding at Cana two thousand years ago!

Action Step

CONSIDER GETTING YOURSELF a scapular, Miraculous Medal, or other Marian sacramental. A sacramental is simply a physical item that reminds us of a deeper spiritual reality and helps us to open up our hearts to receive grace from God. Rosaries, holy water, sacred art and music, and items such as the scapular or saint medals are all considered sacramentals. Remember — it is not the items themselves that have any sort of special intrinsic power. Rather, they help us to be open to allowing God to be more active in our lives.

The promise of a happy death in the arms of Mary or of an outpouring of miraculous grace upon our lives is a sure way to strengthen our faith, hope, and love in Jesus our redeemer. At the end of the day, growing in this manner is the heart of what these devotions and of all other sacramentals are about — loving God more and having greater faith and hope in him. Use the space below to write out your plan for incorporating more sacramentals such as the scapular and Miraculous Medal in your life.

Going Deeper

IN ADDITION TO the brown scapular and Miraculous Medal, we can use many other sacramentals to help us grow in a relationship with Mary and allow her to lead us closer to Christ. For example, putting an icon or some sacred art that depicts the Blessed Mother up in our home can be a great way to draw our awareness to her presence, along with that of her son. A book titled *Compendium of Marian Devotions,* written and compiled by Fr. Ed Broom, is worth investigating if you'd like to learn more about these or other Marian devotions or sacramentals.

Day 40

Marian Consecration

PUT IN ITS simplest terms, Marian consecration is giving oneself completely to the Blessed Mother and asking her to form you into the most perfect version of yourself possible for God. In order to truly comprehend Marian consecration, we need to first understand two fundamental truths: (1) "Jesus wants to include all of us in his work of salvation"[48] and (2) "While everyone is called to lend a hand in the great work of salvation, not everyone has the same role."[49]

In the Gospels, Jesus is constantly empowering His apostles and other followers to share His work in spreading the gospel. From the commissioning to the seventy-two (Luke 10:1–23), to the Great Commission of the apostles at His ascension (Matt. 28:16–20), to the call of St. Paul (Acts 9:1–19), Jesus is constantly sending people out to build up the Church. He tells us in Scripture that the "harvest is plentiful, but the laborers are few" (Matt. 9:37, RSVCE), and expects us to be instruments in spreading the gospel here on earth.

That being said, and as mentioned above, not everyone is called to the same role. Some of us serve as writers or speakers, some are teachers, some build the kingdom primarily through their family life

48 Michael Gaitley, *33 Days to Morning Glory: A Do-It-Yourself Retreat in Preparation for Marian Consecration* (Stockbridge, MA: Marian Press, 2011), 24.

49 Gaitley, *33 Days to Morning Glory,* 24.

and witness. But Mary has a much bigger role than any other saint in helping Jesus build up the Church. She was the first intercessor at the wedding in Cana, where her request to Jesus kickstarted His public ministry (see John 2:1–7). Then, at the Cross, Jesus gave Mary to the Church and the Church to Mary through the beloved disciple (see John 19:26). And as the spouse of the Holy Spirit, Mary continuously prays for our sanctification and purification so that we may be more like her son.

How can we allow Mary to lead us to Jesus and help us become more like Him? All it takes is for us to say "yes" to a deeper relationship with her. She is waiting there patiently like the perfect mother that she is, to embrace us and lead us closer to Jesus. Nothing brings her greater joy.

To be consecrated to Mary is to simply give her permission to work in us and form us into saints for her son. It is a beautiful prayer of self-offering, but the real benefit that we find in it is a complete interior transformation. Countless saints have spoken about how going through Marian consecration was a life-changing experience for them, including Mother Teresa and Pope St. John Paul II. If one of the key purposes of prayer is to make us more perfect and help us grow closer to God, there is perhaps no faster route to take than by consecrating ourselves fully to Jesus through Mary. Hail Holy Queen!

✎ Action Step ✎

SPEND TIME RESEARCHING Marian consecration and praying about whether God is calling you to it in this season of your life. If you feel like He is, I encourage you to get a book about Marian consecration and read it after you finish this book. If you don't feel called to do this at this time, simply take a moment to thank Jesus for sharing His mother with the Church, and make a simple prayer asking Mary to lead you closer to God and help you grow in virtue.

Going Deeper

33 DAYS TO Morning Glory by Fr. Michael Gaitley is the best place to start for anyone looking to learn more about Marian consecration or go through the process for the first time. *True Devotion* by St. Louis de Montfort is also fantastic, but is more demanding in terms of time spent reading, reflecting, and praying. *Led by the Immaculata* by Joshua Mazrin is another excellent Marian consecration option through the lens of St. Maximillian Kolbe's Marian theology.

PART 12

Conclusion — Continuing to Build a Vibrant Prayer Life

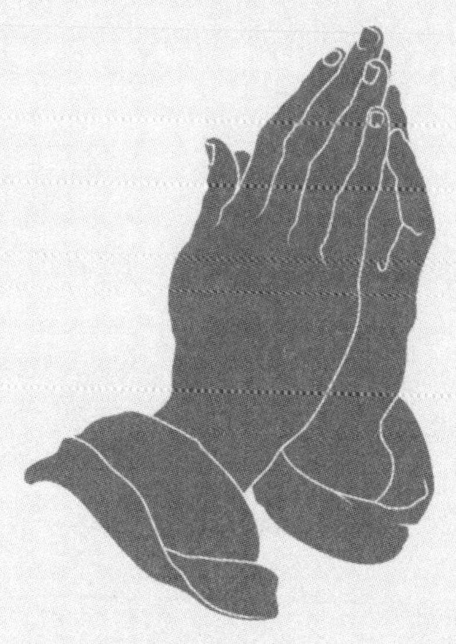

I HOPE THAT spiritually traveling together through these last forty days has been a fruitful experience for you. I am sure that some of the exercises were more beneficial than others for you, and I want to reiterate again that *that's the whole point of this book*! Above all, I hope that this journey inspired in you a deeper love for prayer and that you discovered some methods and forms of prayer that will help you continue to grow closer to God in the months and years to come.

When it comes to building a prayer life, consistency and authenticity are the two most important traits. You have to continue to make the time for prayer, and you need to fully engage in it! You have a spiritual enemy that doesn't want you to pray, but as we've experienced, prayer is *so important* to our spiritual life and our relationship with God. It's crucial that you make a prayer plan as you move forward. As the saying goes, "Failing to plan is planning to fail." You need to make sure you are showing up for your prayer time, and when you do, you have to honestly open up your heart to God, placing yourself in His presence. You have to allow Him to raise to the surface the things in your heart that He wants to bring to light and heal.

As you begin praying more often, you'll find that distractions strike just as you are finally getting your mind to quiet down. All of the little to-dos that you never wrote down will suddenly pop into your head, or you'll find yourself starting to daydream. We are human, and these little distractions are bound to happen. When they do, there are two extremes that we want to avoid: giving into the daydreaming or starting to be hard on ourselves. Acknowledge the distraction, then simply allow it to float away. If you need to, you can write it down so that you can come back to it after prayer, especially if it's something important that you need to remember.

Another issue is how we should respond when God doesn't answer our prayers in the way we hoped, especially when it comes to some sort of tragedy or something we really need but don't receive. It's not easy to continue trusting God when a loved one passes away or we feel our financial security slipping away. I can't give a perfect answer, but when you find yourself in a situation like this where you are upset with God or have struggled to trust in His goodness, I invite you to take Romans 8:28 into prayer: "We know that in everything God works for good with those who love him" (RSVCE).

Ultimately, God wants your perfect happiness and the perfect happiness of everyone you've ever loved. His desire is for you to spend an eternity in joyful communion with Him. While suffering is a natural part of life, we have a God who chose to enter into suffering with us. He doesn't *end* suffering, He redeems it. When Jesus walked the earth, He experienced the loss of loved ones. He wept at the death of Lazarus. He also must have wept at the death of His earthly father, St. Joseph. And He took on some of the greatest physical suffering when He underwent His crucifixion and death. In addition, the Blessed Mother suffered greatly when she saw her only son killed by the Roman executioners. She empathizes with our pain and longs to console us.

The mystery of suffering and its existence is hard to grasp, and we may at times wrestle with God when we go through it in some way. But we need to recognize that God doesn't stand at a distance. God suffers alongside us. He hurts when we hurt, every single time. He is with us in our darkest moments, and He doesn't allow them to be the end of our story. I repeat again, "We know that in everything God works for good for those who love Him." Keep praying through your suffering, and even though you will suffer in this life, you'll know in your heart that God He is with you every step of the way.

Finally, before putting this book down , I'd like you to take some time to write out a prayer game plan for the next one to three months. What time of day are you going to take your prayer time? How long will you pray for? Treat this time as if it is a sort of appointment with God that you need to keep, as if it were an important meeting or any other appointment that we show up for. In fact, time in prayer is your *most important* appointment. What types of prayer from this book are you going to commit to? What types of prayer do you want to revisit and try again sometime or in another season of life? What is God calling you to? One final time, I invite you to use the space below to journal and write your thoughts and game plan.

Thank you for taking this journey with me. Please pray for me and everyone else who has made this forty-day prayer journey, and for anyone else who will make it in the future. Remember, your prayer time can take all sorts of shapes and sizes. In this book, we've explored forty of them, but these are really just a starting point. Talk to God, listen to God, spend time with God. At the end of the day, that is what prayer is all about.

Appendices

A. List of Common Vocal Prayers

B. Examination of Conscience

C. Further Reading for Spiritual Growth

D. St. Ignatius's Rules for Discernment

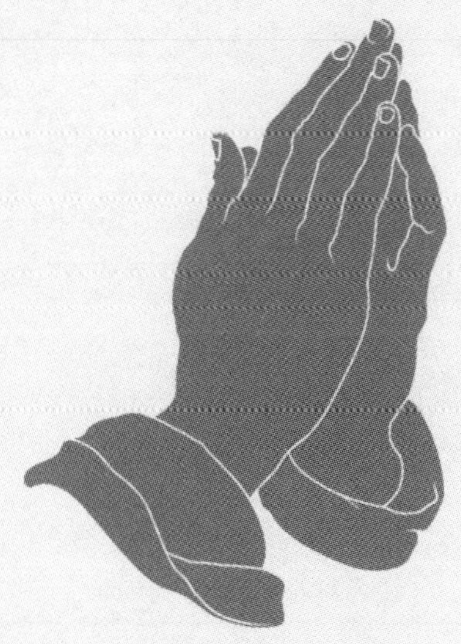

APPENDIX A

List of Common Vocal Prayers

The Sign of the Cross — In the name of the Father, and of the Son, and of the Holy Spirit. Amen.

Our Father — Our Father, Who art in heaven, hallowed be Thy name; Thy kingdom come; Thy will be done on earth as it is in heaven. Give us this day our daily bread; and forgive us our trespasses as we forgive those who trespass against us; and lead us not into temptation, but deliver us from evil. Amen.

Hail Mary — Hail Mary, full of grace, the Lord is with thee; blessed art thou among women and blessed is the fruit of thy womb, Jesus. Holy Mary, Mother of God, pray for us sinners, now and at the hour of our death. Amen.

Glory Be — Glory be to the Father, and to the Son, and to the Holy Spirit; as it was in the beginning, is now, and ever shall be. Amen.

Fatima Prayer (said at the end of decades of the Rosary) — O my Jesus, forgive us our sins; save us from the fires of hell, and lead all souls to heaven, especially those in most need of Your Mercy. Amen.

Hail Holy Queen — Hail, Holy Queen, Mother of Mercy, our life, our sweetness and our hope. To thee do we cry, poor banished children of Eve. To thee do we send up our sighs, mourning and weeping in this valley of tears. Turn then, most gracious advocate, thine eyes of mercy toward us, and after this our exile show unto us the blessed fruit of thy womb, Jesus. O clement, O loving, O sweet Virgin Mary. Pray for us, O most holy Mother of God, that we may be made worthy of the promises of Christ. Amen.

Prayer at the End of the Rosary — Let us pray. O God, whose only-begotten Son, by His life, death, and resurrection, has purchased for us the rewards of eternal life; grant, we beseech Thee, that, meditating upon these mysteries of the Most Holy Rosary of the Blessed Virgin

Mary, we may imitate what they contain and obtain what they promise, through the same Christ our Lord. Amen.

Memorare to the Blessed Mother — Remember, O most gracious Virgin Mary, that never was it known that anyone who fled to thy protection, implored thy help, or sought thy intercession, was left unaided. Inspired by this confidence I fly unto thee, O Virgin of virgins, my Mother. To thee do I come, before thee I stand, sinful and sorrowful. O Mother of the Word Incarnate, despise not my petitions, but in thy mercy hear and answer me. Amen.

Anima Christi — Soul of Christ, sanctify me. Body of Christ, save me. Blood of Christ, inebriate me. Water from the side of Christ, wash me. Passion of Christ, strengthen me. O good Jesus, hear me. Within Your wounds hide me. Never permit me to be parted from You. From the evil Enemy defend me. At the hour of my death call me and bid me come to You, that with Your Saints I may praise You for age upon age. Amen.

Morning Offering — O Jesus, through the Immaculate Heart of Mary, I offer You my prayers, works, joys, and sufferings of this day for all the intentions of Your Sacred Heart in union with the Holy Sacrifice of the Mass throughout the world, for the salvation of souls, the reparation of sins, the reunion of all Christians, and in particular for the intentions of the Holy Father this month. Amen.

Prayer to the Holy Spirit — Come, Holy Spirit, fill the hearts of Your faithful. Enkindle in them the fire of Your love. Send forth Your Spirit and they shall be created and You will renew the face of the earth. Amen.

Divine Praises — Blessed be God. Blessed be His Holy Name. Blessed be Jesus Christ, true God and true Man. Blessed be the Name of Jesus. Blessed be His most Sacred Heart. Blessed be His most Precious Blood. Blessed be Jesus in the most Holy Sacrament of the Altar. Blessed be the Holy Spirit, the Paraclete. Blessed be the great Mother of God, Mary most holy. Blessed be her holy and Immaculate Conception. Blessed be her glorious Assumption. Blessed be the name of Mary, Virgin and Mother. Blessed be St. Joseph, her most chaste spouse. Blessed be God in His angels and in His saints.

Prayer for Vocations — God our Father, we thank You for calling men and women to serve in Your Son's kingdom as priests, deacons, and consecrated persons. Send Your Holy Spirit to help others to respond generously and courageously to Your call. May our community of faith support vocations of sacrificial love in our youth and young adults. Through our Lord Jesus Christ, who lives and reigns with You in the unity of the Holy Spirit, one God, forever and ever. Amen.

Prayer in Times of Financial Struggles — God of mercy and compassion, You promise to give us all that we need. As we face this time of financial struggle, help us to trust in Your providence and keep our hearts fixed on the treasures of heaven. We ask this through Christ our Lord. Amen.

Memorare to St. Joseph — Remember, O most chaste spouse of the Virgin Mary, that never was it known that anyone who implored your help and sought your intercession were left unassisted. Full of confidence in your power I fly unto you and beg your protection. Despise not, O Guardian of the Redeemer, my humble supplication, but in your bounty, hear and answer me. Amen.

St. Michael Prayer — St. Michael the Archangel, defend us in battle. Be our protection against the wickedness and snares of the devil; May God rebuke him, we humbly pray; And do thou, O Prince of the Heavenly Host, by the power of God, thrust into hell Satan and all evil spirits who wander through the world for the ruin of souls. Amen.

Prayer to Our Guardian Angel — Angel of God, my guardian dear, to whom God's love commits me here, ever this day be at my side, to light and guard, to rule and guide. Amen.

The Magnificat — My soul proclaims the greatness of the Lord, my spirit rejoices in God my Savior, for He has looked with favor on His lowly servant. From this day all generations will call me blessed: the Almighty has done great things for me, and holy is His Name. He has mercy on those who fear Him in every generation. He has shown the strength of His arm, He has scattered the proud in their conceit. He has cast down the mighty from their thrones, and has lifted up the lowly. He has filled the hungry with good things, and the rich He has sent away empty. He has come to the help of His servant Israel for He has remembered His promise of mercy, the promise He made to our fathers, to Abraham and to His children forever. Amen.

Act of Faith — O my God, I firmly believe that You are one God in three divine Persons, Father, Son, and Holy Spirit. I believe that Your divine Son became man and died for our sins and that He will come to judge the living and the dead. I believe these and all the truths which the holy catholic church teaches because You have revealed them who are eternal truth and wisdom, who can neither deceive nor be deceived. In this faith I intend to live and die. Amen.

Act of Hope — O Lord God, I hope by Your grace for the pardon of all my sins and after life here to gain eternal happiness because You have promised it who are infinitely powerful, faithful, kind, and merciful. In this hope I intend to live and die. Amen.

Act of Love — O Lord God, I love You above all things and I love my neighbor for Your sake because You are the highest, infinite, and perfect good, worthy of all my love. In this love I intend to live and die. Amen.

Act of Contrition — My God, I am sorry for my sins with all my heart. In choosing to do wrong and failing to do good, I have sinned against You whom I should love above all things. I firmly intend, with Your help, to do penance, to sin no more, and to avoid whatever leads me to sin. Our Savior Jesus Christ suffered and died for us. In His name, my God, have mercy. Amen.

Grace before Meals — Bless us, O Lord, and these Your gifts, which we are about to receive, from Your bounty, through Christ, Our Lord. Amen.

APPENDIX B

Examination of Conscience

(Based on the Ten Commandments)

I. "I am the Lord, thy God, thou shalt not have strange gods before Me."

Have I sinned against Religion by seriously believing in New Age, Scientology, Astrology, Horoscopes, Fortune-telling, Superstition or engaging in the Occult? Did I endanger my Catholic Faith or cause scandal by associating with anti-Catholic groups & associations (e.g., the Freemasons)? Have fame, fortune, money, career, pleasure, etc. replaced God as my highest priority? Have I neglected my daily prayers?

II. "Thou shalt not take the name of the Lord thy God in vain."

Have I committed blasphemy by using the name of God and Jesus Christ to swear rather than to praise? Have I committed sacrilege by showing disrespect to holy objects (crucifix, rosary) or contempt for religious persons (bishop, priests, deacons, women religious) or for sacred places (in Church). Have I committed sacrilege by going to Holy Communion in the state of mortal sin without first going to confession e.g., after missing Mass on Sunday or a Holyday? Did I violate the one-hour fast before Communion? Did I break the laws of fast and abstinence during Lent? Did I neglect my Easter duty to receive Holy Communion at least once? Have I neglected to support the Church and the poor by sharing my time, talent and treasure?

III. Remember to keep holy the Sabbath day.

Did I miss Mass on *any* Sunday or Holyday of Obligation? (Bad weather and being sick do not count) Have I shown disrespect by leaving Mass early, not paying attention or not joining in the prayers? Did I do unnecessary work on Sunday which could have been done the day before? Have I been stingy in my support for the Church? Do I give of my time & talent?

IV. Honor thy father and mother.

Parents: Have I set a bad example for my children by casually missing Mass, neglecting prayer, or ignore my responsibility to provide a Catholic education by either sending my children to parochial school or to C.C.D. (Religious Education Program)? Do I show little or no interest in my children's faith and practice of it? Have I showed disrespect for those in authority, government or church? Have I not expressed my moral values to them?

Children: Have I been disobedient and/or disrespectful to my parents or guardians? Did I neglect to help them with household chores? Have I caused them unnecessary worry and anxiety by my attitude, behavior, moods, etc.?

V. Thou shalt not kill.

Did I consent, recommend, advise, approve, support or have an abortion? Did I realize that there is an excommunication for anyone who procures an abortion? Did I actively or passively cooperate with an act of euthanasia whereby ordinary means were stopped or means taken to directly end the life of an elderly or sick person? Have I committed an act of violence or abuse (physical, sexual, emotional or verbal)? Have I endangered the lives of others by reckless driving or by driving under the influence of drugs or alcohol? Do I show contempt for my body by neglecting to take care of my own health? Have I been mean or unjust to anyone? Have I held a grudge or sought revenge against someone who wronged me? Do I point out others' faults and mistakes while ignoring my own? Do I complain more than I compliment? Am I ungrateful for what other people do for me? Do I tear people down rather than encourage them? Am I prejudiced against people because of their color, language or ethnic-religious background?

VI. Thou shalt not commit adultery.

IX. Thou shalt not covet thy neighbor's wife.

Did I have any sex before or outside of marriage? Do I view pornographic material (magazines, videos, internet, hot-lines)? Have I gone to massage parlors or adult book stores? Did I commit the sins of masturbation and/or artificial contraception? Have I not avoided the occasions of sin (persons or places) which would tempt me to be unfaithful to my spouse or to my own chastity? Do I encourage and entertain impure thoughts and desires? Do I tell or listen to dirty jokes? Have I committed fornication or adultery?

VII. Thou shalt not steal.

X. Thou shalt not covet thy neighbor's goods.

Have I stolen any object, committed any shoplifting or cheated anyone of their money? Did I knowingly deceive someone in business or commit fraud? Have I shown disrespect or even contempt for other people's property? Have I done any acts of vandalism? Am I greedy or envious of another's goods? Do I let financial and material concerns or the desire for comfort override my duty to God, to Church, to my family or my own spiritual well-being?

VIII. Thou shalt not bear false witness against thy neighbor.

Have I told a lie in order to deceive someone? Have I told the truth with the purpose and intention of ruining someone's reputation (sin of detraction)? Have I told a lie or spread rumors which may ruin someone's reputation (sin of calumny or slander)? Did I commit perjury by false swearing an oath on the Bible? Am I a busybody or do I love to spread gossip and secrets about others? Do I love to hear bad news about my enemies?

(Father John Trigilio, Sacrament of Penance: Examination of Conscience, https://www.ewtn.com/catholicism/library/sacrament-of-penance-examination-of-conscience-9121.)

APPENDIX C

Further Reading for Spiritual Growth

- ✠ *Abandonment to Divine Providence* by Jean-Pierre de Caussade
- ✠ *The Ascent of Mount Carmel* by St. John of the Cross
- ✠ *Bible Basics for Catholics* by John Bergsma
- ✠ *Confessions* by St. Augustine
- ✠ *The Dialogue of St. Catherine of Siena* by St. Catherine of Siena
- ✠ *The Diary of St. Faustina* by St. Faustina
- ✠ *The Everlasting Man* by G. K. Chesterton
- ✠ *The Flame of Love* by St. John of the Cross
- ✠ *The Imitation of Christ* by Thomas à Kempis
- ✠ *In the School of the Holy Spirit* by Jacques Philippe
- ✠ *Interior Castle* by St. Teresa of Ávila
- ✠ *Interior Freedom* by Jacques Philippe
- ✠ *Introduction to the Devout Life* by St. Francis de Sales
- ✠ *Jesus of Nazareth* by Pope Benedict XVI
- ✠ *The Journey of the Mind (or "Soul") to God* by St. Bonaventure (also called the Itinerarium)

- ✠ *Let the Fire Fall* by Michael Scanlon
- ✠ *Life of Christ* by Fulton J. Sheen
- ✠ *The Practice of the Presence of God* by Brother Lawrence
- ✠ *The Return of the Prodigal Son* by Henri Nouwen
- ✠ *The Rule of St. Benedict* by St. Benedict of Nursia
- ✠ *Searching for and Maintaining Peace* by Jacques Philippe
- ✠ *The Secret of the Rosary* by St. Louis de Montfort
- ✠ *The Seven Storey Mountain* by Thomas Merton
- ✠ *The Soul of the Apostolate* by Jean-Baptiste Chautard
- ✠ *The Spiritual Combat* by Lorenzo Scupoli
- ✠ *The Spiritual Exercises* by St. Ignatius of Loyola
- ✠ *Story of a Soul* by St. Thérèse of Lisieux
- ✠ *Theology for Beginners* by Frank Sheed
- ✠ *Time for God* by Jacques Philippe
- ✠ *To Know Christ Jesus* by Frank Sheed
- ✠ *Transformation in Christ* by Dietrich von Hildebrand
- ✠ *True Devotion to Mary* by St. Louis de Montfort

APPENDIX D

St. Ignatius's Rules for Discernment

NOTE: THESE RULES were written by St. Ignatius as part of the *Spiritual Exercises*.[50] Some of the language within them is reflective of the time period in which St. Ignatius wrote. Some metaphorical language may seem off-putting to modern ears (especially in Rule 12) but the spiritual meaning is still able to be grasped.

First Rule. The first rule: in persons who are going from mortal sin to mortal sin, the enemy is ordinarily accustomed to propose apparent pleasures to them, leading them to imagine sensual delights and pleasures in order to hold them more and make them grow in their vices and sins. In these persons the good spirit uses a contrary method, stinging and biting their consciences through their rational power of moral judgment.

Second Rule. The second: in persons who are going on intensely purifying their sins and rising from good to better in the service of God our Lord, the method is contrary to that in the first rule. For then it is proper to the evil spirit to bite, sadden, and place obstacles, disquieting with false reasons, so that the person may not go forward. And it is proper to the good spirit to give courage and strength, consolations, tears, inspirations, and quiet, easing and taking away all obstacles, so that the person may go forward in doing good.

[50] *The Spiritual Exercises of St. Ignatius,* trans. Elder Mullan, My Catholic Life!, accessed November 27, 2024, https://mycatholic.life/books/the-spiritual-exercises-of-saint-ignatius-of-loyola/rules/#:~:text=The%20first%20Rule%3A%20In%20the,in%20their%20vices%20and%20sins.

Third Rule. The third is of spiritual consolation. I call it consolation when some interior movement is caused in the soul, through which the soul comes to be inflamed with love of its Creator and Lord, and consequently when it can love no created thing on the face of the earth in itself, but only in the Creator of them all. Likewise, when it sheds tears that move to love of its Lord, whether out of sorrow for one's sins, or for the passion of Christ our Lord, or because of other things directly ordered to His service and praise. Finally, I call consolation every increase of hope, faith, and charity, and all interior joy that calls and attracts to heavenly things and to the salvation of one's soul, quieting it and giving it peace in its Creator and Lord.

Fourth Rule. The fourth is of spiritual desolation. I call desolation all the contrary of the third rule, such as darkness of soul, disturbance in it, movement to low and earthly things, disquiet from various agitations and temptations, moving to lack of confidence, without hope, without love, finding oneself totally slothful, tepid, sad, and as if separated from one's Creator and Lord. For just as consolation is contrary to desolation, in the same way the thoughts that come from consolation are contrary to the thoughts that come from desolation.

Fifth Rule. The fifth: in time of desolation never make a change but be firm and constant in the proposals and determination in which one was the day preceding such desolation, or in the determination in which one was in the preceding consolation. Because, as in consolation the good spirit guides and counsels us more, so in desolation the bad spirit, with whose counsels we cannot find the way to a right decision.

Sixth Rule. The sixth: although in desolation we should not change our first proposals, it is very advantageous to change ourselves intensely against the desolation itself, as by insisting more upon prayer, meditation, upon much examination, and upon extending ourselves in some suitable way of doing penance.

Seventh Rule. The seventh: let one who is in desolation consider how the Lord has left him in trial in his natural powers, so that he may resist the various agitations and temptations of the enemy; since he can resist with the divine help, which always remains with him, though he does not clearly feel it; for the Lord has taken away from him his great fervor, abundant love and intense grace, leaving him, however, sufficient grace for eternal salvation.

Eighth Rule. The eighth: let one who is in desolation work to be in patience, which is contrary to the vexations which come to him, and let him think that he will soon be consoled, diligently using the means against such desolation, as is said in the sixth rule.

Ninth Rule. The ninth: there are three principal causes for which we find ourselves desolate. The first is because we are tepid, slothful, or negligent in our spiritual exercises, and so through our faults spiritual consolation withdraws from us. The second, to try us and see how much we are and how much we extend ourselves in His service and praise without so much payment of consolations and increased graces. The third, to give us true recognition and understanding so that we may interiorly feel that it is not ours to attain or maintain increased devotion, intense love, tears, or any other spiritual consolation, but that all is the gift and grace of God our Lord, and so that we may not build a nest in something belonging to another, raising our mind in some pride or vainglory, attributing to ourselves the devotion or the other parts of the spiritual consolation.

Tenth Rule. The tenth: let the one who is in consolation think how he will conduct himself in the desolation which will come after, taking new strength for that time.

Eleventh Rule. The eleventh: let one who is consoled seek to humble himself and lower himself as much as he can, thinking of how little he is capable of in the time of desolation without such grace or consolation. On the contrary, let one who is in desolation think that he can do much with God's sufficient grace to resist all his enemies, taking strength in his Creator and Lord.

Twelfth Rule. The twelfth: the enemy acts like a woman in being weak when faced with strength and strong when faced with weakness. For, as it is proper to a woman, when she is fighting with some man, to lose heart and to flee when the man confronts her firmly, and, on the contrary, if the man begins to flee, losing heart, the anger, vengeance, and ferocity of the woman grow greatly and know no bounds, in the same way, it is proper to the enemy to weaken and lose heart, fleeing and ceasing his temptations when the person who is exercising himself in spiritual things confronts the temptations of the enemy firmly, doing what is diametrically opposed to them; and, on the contrary, if the person who is exercising himself begins to be afraid and lose heart in suffering the temptations, there is no beast so fierce on the face of the earth as the enemy of human nature in following out his damnable intention with such growing malice.

Thirteenth Rule. The thirteenth: likewise he conducts himself as a false lover in wishing to remain secret and not be revealed. For a dissolute man who, speaking with evil intention, makes dishonorable advances to a daughter of a good father or a wife of a good husband, wishes his words and persuasions to be secret, and the contrary displeases him very much, when the daughter reveals to her father or the wife to her husband his false words and depraved intention, because he easily perceives that he will not be able to succeed with the undertaking begun. In the same way, when the enemy of human nature brings his wiles and persuasions to the just soul, he wishes and desires that they be received and kept in secret; but when one reveals them to one's good confessor or to another spiritual person, who knows his deceits and malicious designs, it weighs on him very much, because he perceives that he will not be able to succeed with the malicious undertaking he has begun, since his manifest deceits have been revealed.

Fourteenth Rule. The fourteenth: likewise, he conducts himself as a leader, intent upon conquering and robbing what he desires. For, just as a captain and leader of an army in the field, pitching his camp and exploring the fortifications and defenses of a stronghold, attacks it at the weakest point, in the same way the enemy of human nature, roving about, looks in turn at all our theological, cardinal, and moral virtues; and where he finds us weakest and most in need for our eternal salvation, there he attacks us and attempts to take us.

About the Author

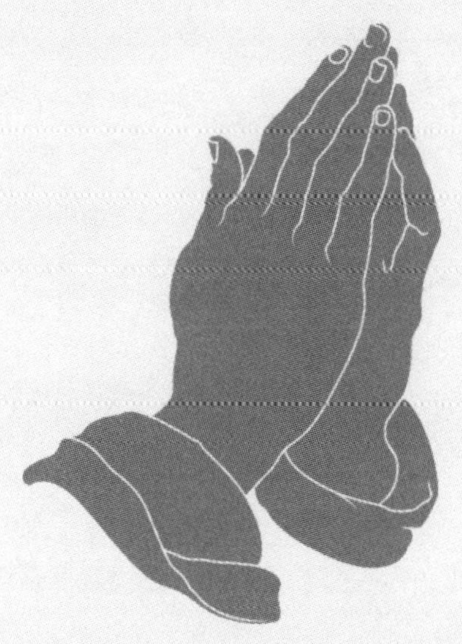

About the Author

Jonah Paul Soucy is a Catholic speaker, musician, and author who hails from the wonderful Catholic community of Pittsburgh, Pennsylvania. At a young age, Jonah experienced God in a powerful way through the beauty of the White Mountains of New Hampshire, the state where he grew up. As he grew older, he experienced God more fully through encountering Him in Eucharistic Adoration and in prayer. Currently serving as a youth minister in the Diocese of Pittsburgh, Jonah recently received a Master of Arts in Catechetics and Evangelization from Franciscan University. He lives in the South Hills of Pittsburgh with his wife, Shannon, and their son, Aiden.

MY THOUGHTS AND REFLECTIONS

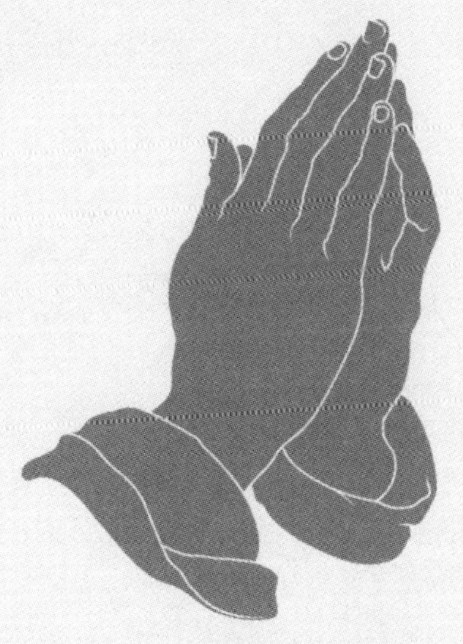

MY THOUGHTS AND REFLECTIONS

MY THOUGHTS AND REFLECTIONS

MY THOUGHTS AND REFLECTIONS

MY THOUGHTS AND REFLECTIONS

MY THOUGHTS AND REFLECTIONS

MY THOUGHTS AND REFLECTIONS

MY THOUGHTS AND REFLECTIONS

Sophia Institute

SOPHIA INSTITUTE IS a nonprofit institution that seeks to nurture the spiritual, moral, and cultural life of souls and to spread the gospel of Christ in conformity with the authentic teachings of the Roman Catholic Church.

Sophia Institute Press fulfills this mission by offering translations, reprints, and new publications that afford readers a rich source of the enduring wisdom of mankind.

Sophia Institute also operates the popular online resource CatholicExchange.com. *Catholic Exchange* provides world news from a Catholic perspective as well as daily devotionals and articles that will help readers to grow in holiness and live a life consistent with the teachings of the Church.

In 2013, Sophia Institute launched Sophia Institute for Teachers to renew and rebuild Catholic culture through service to Catholic education. With the goal of nurturing the spiritual, moral, and cultural life of souls, and an abiding respect for the role and work of teachers, we strive to provide materials and programs that are at once enlightening to the mind and ennobling to the heart; faithful and complete, as well as useful and practical.

Sophia Institute gratefully recognizes the Solidarity Association for preserving and encouraging the growth of our apostolate over the course of many years. Without their generous and timely support, this book would not be in your hands.

www.SophiaInstitute.com
www.CatholicExchange.com
www.SophiaTeachers.org

Sophia Institute Press is a registered trademark of Sophia Institute.
Sophia Institute is a tax-exempt institution as defined by the
Internal Revenue Code, Section 501(c)(3). Tax ID 22-2548708.